MUSIC & DRAMA LIBRARY
TROW. 3641 EXT. 2713

-2. JAN. 1986
18. NOV. 1987
23. NOV. 1988
AS→CR 23/9/88
22.
Ex loan 3/12/88
12. NOV 88
16. 1989
16. JUN. 1989

IBL→CI
30 MAR 1990
19. FEB. 1990
13. MAR. 1990
30 APR 1992
30 JUL 1992

# Let's Dance – Country Style

A handbook of simple, traditional dances

REVISED EDITION

**Ronald Smedley and John Tether**

*Illustrations by Rowland Howls*

*Technical drawings by John Barber*

WILTSHIRE LIBRARY & MUSEUM SERVICE

PAUL ELEK
**GRANADA PUBLISHING**
London Toronto Sydney New York

Granada Publishing Limited
Frogmore, St Albans, Herts AL2 2NF
and
36 Golden Square, London W1R 4AH
866 United Nations Plaza, New York, NY 10017, USA
117 York Street, Sydney, NSW 2000, Australia
100 Skyway Avenue, Rexdale, Ontario M9W 3A6, Canada
61 Beach Road, Auckland, New Zealand

First published by Paul Elek Books Ltd 1972
Reprinted 1976
Revised edition published by Granada Publishing in Paul Elek Ltd 1981
Reprinted 1982

Copyright © Ronald Smedley, John Tether 1972, 1981
The copyright in the illustrations is held by Rowland Howls and John Barber

ISBN 0 246 11541 6

Printed in Great Britain by
Richard Clay (The Chaucer Press) Ltd,
Bungay, Suffolk

All rights reserved. No part of this publication may be reproduced, stored in a retrieval system, or transmitted, in any form or by any means, electronic, mechanical, photocopying, recording or otherwise, without the prior permission of the publishers.

Granada ®
Granada Publishing ®

# Contents

# Acknowledgments

The people who have contributed towards this book are far too numerous to mention individually, even if we knew all their names, for they are the many thousands of dancers, young and old alike, who have given us so many pleasurable evenings up and down the country. From the school-dinner ladies of Barking with their husbands to the villagers of Cartmel and Widecombe – we thank them all.

Particular thanks are due to Nora Dean, who translated our illegible scrawl into a beautifully neat typescript, to Roland Howls for his delightful drawings of the dancers, to John Barber for his excellent technical illustrations, and to Alan Platt for transcribing the music.

R. S. J. T.

# Introduction

## WHAT THE BOOK IS ABOUT

We're not evangelists: we're not trying to sell you a magic formula for dancing that is better than any other sort of dancing. The world is a big place and there's plenty of room for everything – ballroom, old-time, beat or ballet. But there do seem times when there's something missing from public dancing today – a guaranteed sociability where the dancing provides a real opportunity for people to enjoy the company of everybody else in the hall.

If this book is about anything, it is about that. It describes dances that are for groups of people, together; dances that are so simple that everyone can do them, but *real* dances, not party games.

You must think of a hall packed with people; all sorts of people, young and old. The music is good and strong and loud enough without being ear-shattering. There's plenty to eat and drink. People actually seem to be cheerful and enjoying themselves and most of the men have their coats off. They applaud, noisily, when the dances finish and they come out smiling ready for the next one.

Now there aren't many dance-halls where that happens. But this can happen, it does happen and we've made it happen. Whether it happens depends very largely on the skill of the leader of the evening (the M.C. or Master of Ceremonies – a dance teacher in disguise), in conjunction with good music. And this book is really for the would-be M.C. or leader who either wants to run dance evenings for pleasure or profit or who, perhaps, is already helping to run a club – any sort of club – and who wants to introduce something fresh.

It is a book for youth leaders or teachers in secondary schools; it is for parents' associations, church clubs, Rotary clubs, social secretaries, sports clubs and wine guilds. It is for anybody, really, who likes helping other people to have a good time.

It is also for those who would like to learn something about how to do these dances. And it is for those who may know a few dances and would like to learn more.

One of us once ran an evening – a fairly short one – for a group of very old ladies, euphemistically assembled as a 'wives' club' in a settlement in the East End of London. At the end of the 'do', which was more of a 'knees-up' than anything else, one of the ladies said: 'At least it's a change from ruddy Bingo!'

At its very least, this book is a change from 'ruddy Bingo'. At its very best, it is an introduction to a stimulating and satisfying dance-form which has its roots in the culture of Western Europe generally and Britain in particular. It is not a specialist's book, it is not necessarily a beginner's book. It is a book for dancers who like to have a good time with their friends – or with anybody, if it comes to that!

Chapter 1

# About the history of the dances we shall use

It is not an easy thing to do, to 'write down' dancing and even now the only really satisfactory way for a dancer to learn is to watch someone else or be taught by a 'live' teacher. For this reason, little was written down in the old days, so we can only guess at how people danced centuries ago. One of the first and most famous books on how to dance was written by a French priest in 1588. He gave himself a pen name, Arbeau, and his famous book, called *Orchésographie*, is written as a conversation between himself and a young man, Capriol, who was keen to know how to get with the contemporary scene. Arbeau told him what to wear, how to behave, how not to eat too much meat in case it made his breath smell – and how to dance. Most of the dances in the book are what we might call open couple dances, where each man has his partner and the steps of the dance are repeated again and again: rather like the Olde Tyme sequence dances that we know today. Most European ladies and gentlemen of the time danced dances like these and had done for several centuries.

Round about the time of Elizabeth I a new diversion, as a contrast to the couple dances, was introduced at court – the dances of the English country-people. They were first danced as entertainment for the Queen, or as part of a play or masque, and later for everybody to join in. The attraction of these country-people's dances was firstly that the music was lively and fairly fast (often it was the pop songs of the time, though pop songs then had a longer life than they do today) and secondly that they were dances for a group of people rather than for couples alone. You still had a partner but you were in a 'set' – a big circle, a long line or a square – with the rest of your friends. There were few steps to remember, if any; the pleasure came from the patterns and figures you made.

These dances, with names like *Trenchmore*, *The Cushion Dance* and *Sellenger's Round*, became popular at all social levels, not only at court but also in the country houses and countryside. Dancing, of course, in those days was far more important for leisured people than it is now.

These 'new' country dances were, in fact, really very old. The country people, dancing hand in hand in a circle made a direct link, in their dancing, with the ceremonial dances of long, long before when the whole community of people danced around a bush or a may-pole or a tree – whatever they held sacred, or around the boundaries of the little cleared and cultivated world in which they lived in the forests of pre-Christian Britain – where the unseen outside world had to be shown, with music, singing and dancing, noise and colour, exactly who lived where.

By the beginning of the seventeenth century the country people's figure dances, by now called Country Dances (with a capital C and D), were appearing in dancing teachers' notebooks. The Victor Sylvesters of the time were already teaching them, and making up new dances in the country style. The first *printed* book of country dances appeared, oddly enough, during the Commonwealth in 1651. It was called *The English Dancing Master* – which was partly a joke because most dancing masters were French – and it was published by a Mr John Playford, who had a shop near St Paul's churchyard in London. It was a great success and he and his sons and nephews brought out many more editions over the next seventy years. Soon there were other publishers on the band-waggon and by the eighteenth century Country Dancing had become the most popular dance style in England. As a fashion it spread into Scotland (after 1700, for before this date dancing was an offence for which you could be arrested), into Wales, Ireland and then through the courts, to the Continent and, with the British settlers, to America. In fact the country dances were England's great contribution to the popular arts of Western Europe.

If you went to a ball night at the Bath Assembly, for instance, you would begin with minuets (each couple dancing in turn, beginning with those of highest social rank – how terrible to be the last couple), then go in to supper, and after that there would be 'naught but country dances'.

Of course nothing lasts for ever, even good things, and after a couple of centuries of country dancing, the leisured classes began to look, understandably perhaps, for something different.

'Oh give me new figures, I can't go on dancing
The ones that were taught me ten seasons ago,
The Schoolmaster over the land is advancing,
So why is the master of dancing so slow?'

As the nineteenth century began, the plea was answered by the most shocking dance that had ever been seen – the *Waltz*. It wasn't the dance that was so disturbing, but the position in which the dancers were required to engage – face to face, quite close and arms round each other's waists. It was a horrifying sight to polite society and an obvious sign of decadence and decaying morals, but it managed to survive and after its arrival in London in 1812 it began, very slowly, to spread. Then came the *Lancers* and *Quadrilles*, the *Polka*, *Mazurka* and *Galop*, and the country dances, having enjoyed a brief flare of popularity after the Napoleonic Wars, began to fall from favour. By mid-century only *Sir Roger de Coverley* was left, to stagger eventually into this century as a finisher at children's parties.

In Scotland and Ireland, however, the dances didn't die but remained very much alive, and in rural England the country people, whose property they'd been in the first place and who were slower to change, kept dancing the figure dances, changing them to suit their own tastes. Many of them survived into this century and were written down by the great folk song and dance collectors of our own times – Cecil Sharp, Maud Karpeles, Peter Kennedy, Tom Flett, and others.

We describe this collected material, seen and written down by our contemporaries, as 'traditional' country dancing to avoid confusing it with the dances in the books and manuscripts of the times between Elizabeth I and the young Victoria, which were far greater in number, but somewhat different in character. It is mostly on these traditional dances that we shall base the practical chapters of our book. They provide simple, up-to-date, lively and first-rate material for any occasion when friends – or strangers – get together. We shall also include some very simple American

Square Dances; they have strong British roots and are similar in style to our own traditional dances.

All the dances in this book are basic, very simple – occasionally even simplified – and are guaranteed foolproof for inexperienced dancers. There are about ten thousand or more dances (and this is an official estimate) that you can go on to enjoy if you want to, some of which are not simple at all. The last chapter in the book will tell you how to take the subject further, if you are interested.

We have both used the dances from this book, and others, in many circumstances and often with remarkable results: we have had Saturday night dances packed to the doors, young and old turned away, and even, in a small Devonshire village, different coloured admission tickets to avoid an unbearable crush on the dance floor ('the next dance will be for pink ticket holders only'); and there have been many much smaller, but just as enjoyable, occasions – maybe in somebody's front room or the old schoolroom, decorated for the annual parent/teachers' get-together. All we've found necessary is good music, a good crowd of ordinary people and a little skill but a lot of sensitivity from the M.C.

We'll try to help you with the skill.

Chapter 2

# Style and dress

Style, as distinct from steps and figures, almost defies verbal description. Style is a thing you have naturally and a thing to be demonstrated visually. To learn what it is, you should really go to some dances, find out who's good and watch them, or better still, dance with them.

But here are a few very general principles about style in country dancing.

**Dance Walk**

There are virtually no 'steps' in this book, everything is just 'walking around' – but that means 'dance walking', not plodding, or marching.

Listen to a march from a military band and watch a troop of soldiers marching. The tune hits the beat with a thump, thump, thump. The soldiers hit the ground in front of them, also, with a thump of the heel and then pull their bodies through and over that leading foot. In other words, they stride out.

But a country dance tune, though it may be in the same tempo as a march doesn't, or shouldn't, have that effect on you. A dance tune doesn't thump the beat dead centre: it makes far more use of the 'off' beat – the cracks between the notes, as it were. It's the off beat that gives the dance tune its kick, its life – its lilt. So a dance tune doesn't make you want to stride out, it makes you want to dance around. It makes children skip about. You are not a child, so you won't skip about – instead you will 'dance walk' to the music. And your dance walk will have the same lilt as the music, the same rise or fall, the 'umti-tumti' quality.

**The back foot not the front foot**

You won't think, like the soldier, of the foot that goes forward, of the heel that digs into the ground in front of you. A dancer thinks more of the foot he leaves behind. He carries the weight of his body over the foot and he leaves the weight on his back foot for as long as he can. That helps to give the dancer's body its lilt, its rise and fall – he's not a marcher but a dancer.

**Walk tall**

But, of course, a good natural dancer thinks of his feet hardly at all. His feet, in a sense, follow his body. A good dancer 'walks tall' and carries himself from the chest and shoulders. (A soldier would do that as well, of course). He feels almost like a puppet on strings must feel. The 'support' comes up in the shoulders and the chest and the body 'hangs' underneath. He 'leads' from the chest and shoulders. In other words you don't slump, your 'carriage' is too good for that. This isn't because it looks good, it's because it makes for good full dancing – dancing which is relaxed yet purposeful.

**So relax!**

A good dancer's body and limbs are relaxed – not floppy, not tense but relaxed. Not tight or constricted, no taut muscles – but working just hard enough. Like any good workman you'll put enough of your body into the job to get the job done. Too much and you waste your energies and don't last the day; too little and the whole job becomes pointless. The men who used to scythe corn by hand all day long could give us the rhythm and effort pattern for good dancing. Beginners, particularly young ones or nervous ones, often put far too much into their dancing and zoom round the room like flies that have been sprayed with fly killer. Relax. Take it easy. Let the music do it for you. The best dancers are often the fat ones, because they *have* to take it easy.

**But, open out**

But relaxing doesn't mean shutting your body down. There are plenty of movements that need your arms to turn your partner round, your hand to hold hers. Nothing looks or feels worse than niggling little movements, particularly in a man.

If you're going to give a hand and an arm to turn your partner (see page 30) – give all your arm, nearly straight up at chest height, nice and springy. Not tense, not floppy but springy. If you're giving a hand, give a hand, not a piece of wet fish. And if you're turning, remember that it's the whole weight of your body transmitted along your arm and hand that makes for the pleasure of the turning.

**And you're looking good**

Remember one thing. These dances are not museum pieces or relics of a cult. They are part of our present and our past and are, and have been, the property of British and American people of all kinds and conditions. They are and have been popular dances and popular dancing is natural dancing.

So if people look weird when they dance it's because they are weird or because they haven't yet got the hang of it. It's nothing to do with the dances. The dances suit hippies, housewives, schoolteachers, Members of Parliament, bus conductors or hop-pickers – they're anybody's.

**The dress for dancing in**

You wear what you want to wear, what you look your best in. We used to know a very distinguished gentleman who looked perfectly respectable and ordinary until it came to a dance. Then he 'had to go off and change': and he would come back like a tramp, as if he were going to dig a particularly unpleasant part of his garden. This is quite unnecessary and insulting to the dances (to say nothing of the rest of the dancers). Men may like to take their jackets off, because there's plenty of full body movement, but it's not essential (and certainly not traditional, as any old countryman would tell you). Women shouldn't wear heels that are too high. Don't wear plimsolls: there's not enough heel. Otherwise, you wear what you think is best for the particular occasion.

This might be the place to clear up a possible misconception. Because you can use the word 'folk' to describe the general origins of the country dance, the material is sometimes confused with the other main stream of folk dance material, the men's ritual dance, sometimes called The Morris Dance. Morris Dancing is for display by specialists and does require a uniform (like hippies and skinheads and punks do) of bright clothes, bells, ribbons, flowers and handkerchiefs. But that sort of dressing-up has nothing at all to do with the country dances in this book.

Because of school-day memories, country dancing is sometimes confused in people's minds with the plaiting of ribbons around a Maypole. This is a completely phoney invention of well-meaning Victorian educationists. There are English maypoles, but they are as tall as telegraph poles and no-one has ever plaited ribbons round them.

In any case our country dances are ballroom dances, not village green dances. They have been ballroom dances for many centuries. Dancing for pleasure out-of-doors in Britain is risky, draughty and vastly over-rated.

Chapter 3

# The music

This chapter is for those who don't know much about music. It contains all a dancer needs to know about country dance music. It is written in layman's terms rather than musician's terms. Musicians may skip to Chapter 4.

You may dance to one musician, a group of musicians or a record player. We shall talk about the music first and the musicians later.

**Reels and Jigs**

Most of the tunes for country dancing are played in a bright lively style, somewhat in the tempo of a march. There are other, slower, rhythms – hornpipes, schottisches and waltzes – but we can ignore them for the moment. These lively, march-like tunes are either reels or jigs.

A reel is a 'flat' sort of tune whereas a jig is 'bumpy'.

A *reel* has a rhythm which sounds something like: rum tum, rum tum, rum tum, rum tum' (the 'rum' has as much emphasis as the 'tum').

| | |
|---|---|
| *Bobby Shaftoe*<br>*Knees Up Mother Brown*<br>*Yankee Doodle*<br>*Coming Round the Mountain* | are (flat) reels |

A *jig* has a 'bumpy' rhythm, which sounds like: R*u*mpety T*u*mpety, R*u*mpety T*u*mpety, R*u*mpety T*u*mpety' (the first syllables are strong, the second are weak).

| | |
|---|---|
| *Cock o' the North*<br>*MacNamara's Band*<br>*Humpty Dumpty sat on the Wall*<br>*Boys and Girls Come out to Play* | are all (bumpy) jigs |

**How to tell a Reel from a Jig**

Say the 'rum tum' sequence to yourself while a tune is being played – remember that the 'rum' must be as strong as the 'tum'.

If you can do that, in time with the tune, then that tune is a reel.

If you get bored with 'Rum tum' try saying 'Crystal Palace' or 'Craven Cottage'; each syllable having equal emphasis.

| | | | | |
|---|---|---|---|---|
| **Tune** | **Yankee** | **Doodle** | **went to** | **London** |
| *say to yourself* | rum tum<br>Cr*y*st*a*l | rum tum<br>P*a*l*a*ce | rum tum<br>Cr*y*st*a*l | rum tum<br>P*a*l*a*ce |
| **Tune** | **riding** | **on a** | **po** | **ny** |
| *yourself* | rum tum<br>Cr*y*st*a*l | rum tum<br>P*a*l*a*ce | rum tum<br>Cr*y*st*a*l | rum tum<br>P*a*l*a*ce |

or

| | | | | |
|---|---|---|---|---|
| **Tune** | **Bobby** | **Shaftoe's** | **gone to** | **sea** |
| *yourself* | rum tum<br>Cr*a*v*e*n | rum tum<br>C*o*tt*a*ge | rum tum<br>Cr*a*v*e*n | rum tum<br>C*o*tt*a*ge |
| **Tune** | **Silver** | **Buckles** | **on his** | **knee** |
| *yourself* | rum tum<br>Cr*a*v*e*n | rum tum<br>C*o*tt*a*ge | rum tum<br>Cr*a*v*e*n | rum tum<br>C*o*tt*a*ge |

You'll find there are some tunes where 'rum tum' doesn't fit, but R*u*mpety T*u*mpety does. These are the jigs.

If you want to stay with the footballers, instead of Rumpety Tumpety, try saying 'L*i*verpool' or '*E*verton' fast, like a tongue twister.

Like this:

| **Tune** | **Oh my** | **name is** | **MacNa** | **mara** |
|---|---|---|---|---|
| *yourself* | | Rumpety<br>L*i*verpool | Tumpety<br>L*i*verpool | Rumpety<br>L*i*verpool |

| **Tune** | **I'm the** | **leader** | **of the** | **band** |
|---|---|---|---|---|
| *yourself* | Rumpety<br>L*i*verpool | Tumpety<br>L*i*verpool | Rumpety<br>L*i*verpool | Tumpety<br>L*i*verpool |

or

| **Tune** | **When** | **I was** | **born ap** | **prentice** | |
|---|---|---|---|---|---|
| *yourself* | | Rumpety<br>*E*verton | Tumpety<br>*E*verton | Rumpety<br>*E*verton | Tumpe<br>*E*vert |

| **Tune** | **in** | **famous** | **Lincoln** | **shire** | |
|---|---|---|---|---|---|
| *yourself* | ty<br>on | Rumpety<br>*E*verton | Tumpety<br>*E*verton | Rumpcty<br>*E*verton | Tumpety<br>*E*verton |

Do you see how a reel is a straightforward, flat tune whereas a jig bumps or ripples along? Try listening to some records until you can distinguish one from the other – you will be using both.

Some dances need reels, some need jigs and some may be danced equally well to either. A jig has a kick to it that makes people pick their feet up, a reel has a drive that pushes people along.

Some M.C.s always have a dance in reel time followed by a dance in jig time (plus waltzes and hornpipes) to vary the atmosphere of the dance.

A jig is sometimes called a 6/8 tune. (That is what is written at the beginning of the music to tell the musician how it should be played. Technically it means that there are six eighth-notes, or quavers, in each bar.)

A reel should have 2/4 or 4/4 written at the beginning of the music (this means that there are two or four quarter-notes, or crotchets, in each bar).

There are also *dances* and *dance figures* (as distinct from *tunes*) which are called reels or jigs. Put those out of your mind for the moment. You have quite enough to think about, as it is.

We have only given examples of well-known, popular tunes in reel-time and jig-time; there are many, many thousands of traditional reels and jigs, some of them very old, many of them beautiful to listen to and some of them as hard to play as Scarlatti or Mozart. But they are all either 'flat' or 'bumpy'. And they are all, with a few exceptions, the same length.

**The length of the tunes**

Technically speaking, almost all country dance *music* is built up of phrases of eight bars.

If you walk around humming any jig or reel, and take sixteen steps, you will have used up eight bars of music.

Do that once or twice, two steps to the bar, and then forget the counting before it becomes a habit.

A reel:

| | | | |
|---|---|---|---|
| **Tune** | **Bobby Shaftoe's** | **gone to sea** | **silver buckles** |
| *Bars of music* | 1st bar | 2nd bar | 3rd bar |
| **Tune** | **on his knee** | | |
| *Bars* | 4th bar | | |

| | | | | |
|---|---|---|---|---|
| **Tune** | **He'll come back and** | **marry me** | **Bonny Bobby** | |
| *Bars* | 5th bar | 6th bar | 7th bar | |
| **Tune** | **Shaftoe** | | | |
| *Bars* | 8th bar | | | |

or a jig:

| | | | | |
|---|---|---|---|---|
| **Tune** | **Humpty Dumpty** | **sat on the wall** | **Humpty Dumpty** | |
| *Bars* | 1st bar | 2nd bar | 3rd bar | |
| **Tune** | **had a great fall** | | | |
| *Bars* | 4th bar | | | |
| **Tune** | **All the King's horses and** | **all the King's men** | | |
| *Bars* | 5th bar | 6th bar | | |
| **Tune** | **couldn't put Humpty to** | **gether again** | | |
| *Bars* | 7th bar | 8th bar | | |

Most country dance figures are completed in four or eight bars.

*To save time and confusing the non-musicians, after this chapter, we will refer to eight bars of music as a 'line' of music, or as a 'line' of dancing. This is entirely our own term; it has no musical respectability at all. You will find the term used throughout this book. A 'line' is the time it takes to play or to dance to eight bars of a standard tune.*

**Sixteen Bars make the Tune**

The eight bars of *Bobby Shaftoe*, that we counted out above, is half the tune; there is another 'line' of eight bars that makes up the second half of the tune.

| | | | | |
|---|---|---|---|---|
| **Tune** | **Bobby Shaftoe** | **bright and fair** | **combing down his** | |
| *Bars* | 9th bar | 10th bar | 11th bar | |
| **Tune** | **yellow hair** | | | |
| *Bars* | 12th bar | | | |
| **Tune** | **He's my ain for** | **ever mair** | **Bonny Bobby** | **Shaftoe** |
| *Bars* | 13th bar | 14th bar | 15th bar | 16th bar |

Now the tune has ended. If you want to sing any more about Bobby Shaftoe, you must go back to the beginning of the tune again.

So, like most country dance tunes, *Bobby Shaftoe* is sixteen bars (or two lines) long.

The first eight bars (one line) could be called the 'A' music.

The second eight bars (one line) could be called the 'B' music.

In fact, if you play a country dance record, you will find that the band usually plays the 'A' music twice (to make sixteen bars) and then plays the 'B' music twice (another sixteen bars) – making a total of thirty-two bars from start to finish of the tune. They then go on, repeating those thirty-two bars (two A's, two B's), either to the end of the track or until they decide to change tunes.

There are tunes that vary. Some have 'C' music or even 'C' and 'D' music. *MacNamara's Band* is like this. Each 'line' (or eight bars) is different from the other. But the tune is still complete in thirty-two bars.

This is very convenient because most country dances are in figures that are completed in thirty-two bars of music, So when the figures start to repeat so does the tune, and vice versa.

There are variations, but to sum up the general principles:

1. Most tunes come in eight-bar phrases.
2. Most tunes are completed in sixteen bars (two lines).
3. Most bands play each set of eight bars twice to make up thirty-two bars (four lines).
4. Most of the sets of figures that make up the dances in this book need thirty-two bars (four lines) of music.
5. So, when the tune starts again, the dance starts again.

**The Musicians**

Traditionally, music to dance to was provided by a single player – a fiddler, a piper, a concertina player – but over the last forty years, country dance bands have appeared. Scotland's Jimmy Shand's is probably the best known.

Good bands, in England anyway, are not all that common, though the standard and quality are steadily rising.

Instrumentally speaking, bands for this type of dancing are not at all like ballroom dance-bands. Usually they are made up of a fiddle (or fiddles), an accordion (or accordions) and a melodeon or concertina, to provide most of the melody, with a selection of guitar, piano, drums, and double bass, to provide most of the rhythm or bass. Piccolos, clarinets, trumpets or flutes may also be used.

You can look at the last chapter in this book to find out possible ways of contacting bands in your area. But if you know of good players who could make up a suitable combination for your dance or club, try it out.

If the dancers are few in number, a solo accordion might be ideal; a solo piano, unless played with great virility, is not the best of instruments, though piano and fiddle (and drums) together can be great.

The players could 'busk' a few tunes like *Cock o' the North*, *Coming Round the Mountain*, or *Yankee Doodle* or try playing from the many books of traditional tunes. But be careful: playing for any sort of dancing is a skilled art and although it is possible to have a good time with a poor M.C., an awful hall, no refreshments or drinks, you can *never* have a good time with bad music. If you can't be sure of good music from a band, then you would be better using records (see Appendix).

But don't be afraid to experiment. We took records to a club once to find that the record player didn't work; so we made do with an old 'beery' piano and a pianist who noisily, but rhythmically, crashed his way through about five tunes – and we had a whale of a time.

But respect your musicians and remember that however simple your demands, they are playing in a great tradition of musicianship that reaches back for hundreds of years.

So, if you are working with a band, treat them well. Warn them, in good time, of what dances you want, and warn them, in good time, when you want each dance to stop. They are your friends and a vital part of the proceedings. Make sure they get their refreshments in the interval before anybody else does – even if they are getting paid for their music.

Chapter 4

# The dances: and how to put them over

There are literally tens of thousands of dances to choose from. Here are seventeen very simple (and occasionally simplified) ones. They require nothing more from the dancers than the ability to walk around and to know their right hand from their left (a word of warning – not everyone does). They are dances for a social occasion and not a dancing class.

We shall describe the dances in detail. We shall also point out some of the pitfalls to beware of when teaching them.

Let's begin by talking about our technique of teaching (or leading) at a dance evening. This technique is one way of making an evening go well with no fuss and no embarrassment. As we are both males we will address you as male – make the adjustment as necessary.

**How to lead the evening**

If you are just a small group of friends in the front room, it doesn't matter what you do: prop up the book on the mantelpiece and have a good laugh if things go wrong.

But if you're going to work with a larger group of people, then you have a responsibility to them to know what you are doing: if things go wrong, it won't be a laugh for long. Read this section through carefully. It is probably better not to attempt to be the leader, or 'caller', until you have some experience with the dances yourself. If you are not familiar with all the material, it's probably best to go through each dance beforehand with a small group of people. If this group comes along with you to the dance, then you might be able to use them to help demonstrate the dances to the rest of the company. But it is not essential.

Let's assume that you are not taking your friends along: there's only you. (This is how we usually work.) Let's assume that there are between fifty and a hundred and fifty people at the dance – you should manage to work with this number easily enough.

There they all are – sitting down, looking at you, waiting to start. (Incidentally, until you've had some practice, keep away from youth clubs, unless you know the kids. They'll sit there waiting to eat you alive. Working with young people needs a well-developed skill, although, of course, it brings very real rewards to the successful.)

If you've got a band, let them play a bit of music to liven up the atmosphere. If you are using recorded music, let some of your most lively tunes play your customers into the hall.

Start the evening off with a dance that is so simple it can't fail. The *Virginia Reel* or the *Big Set* are good examples. The evening can only go well if people trust you, and you need to sow the seeds of trust very early on; so start off cool and easy.

Let's say we've chosen the Virginia Reel. (This is a five-line dance – it is explained more fully on p. 48.) One way we might teach it – without using a demonstration group – is by breaking it down into about ten stages. Of course, it is not intended to be a strict routine with ten obligatory steps nor is it the only way to do it – all callers and M.C.s differ in style to some degree, and *circumstances* are never the same on different occasions. This just indicates the sort of atmosphere in which we work and the principle of 'few words, quick action, basic material'.

**Stages**

1. Without showing anybody anything, get the dancers on to the floor in the correct formation. This is one of the reasons why the *Virginia Reel* is a good dance to start with: the formation is easy to explain and easy to understand (see figure overleaf). You only need to say something like:

'All the men stand in a line on this side and all the ladies in a line on that side, facing their partners, four couples in each set.'

This 'getting all the dancers on the floor' before any sort of demonstration doesn't appeal to all callers or M.C.s. Some prefer to encourage a few people to get up and help them give a picture of the dance while the rest of the company sits and watches: that's fine and you may choose to work that way. (You may certainly like to try this later on in the evening with a dance like

*Waves of Tory*, for instance, which needs a certain amount of explaining.) You may like to work this way if your voice isn't very strong – women callers often don't like to shout over the top of a crowd too much. And, of course, if your crowd is a really large one – several hundreds – then you'll have to 'show it first, all stand up after'. You may feel on such occasions that you need a specially-trained demonstration group.

The method of 'stand up first' is particularly useful where there are not too many people at the dance (or perhaps not everyone has arrived yet but you want to start on time.) Then it's certainly better to get everyone on their feet if you can.

How do they *know* they are going to be able to do what's necessary once they've committed themselves by standing up? They don't – it's just something in your face and the way you talk to them that should give them absolute confidence in you. This requires a bit of practice.

You'll discover, once you get used to it, that you must find the right words to describe what you want in as few words as possible, while still sounding friendly and informal. Don't talk too much. (You'll also make lots of mistakes to begin with. Never mind: just learn, learn, learn from experience.)

2. When you've made up as many sets as you can – and you might need to use a bit of cheerful encouragement to prise people off their chairs to begin with – borrow someone's place at the top of one of the sets in the middle of the floor. Using this set as a demonstration team, show the first 'line' of the dance. (A full description of the dance follows on page 48. Have a look at this before reading on.)

Say: 'Hold hands down the lines; now go *forward and back* twice.' (See glossary of figures, p. 29.)

At this stage we don't use any music. We usually use a sort of 'doodling' with the voice – an 'umti tumti' sort of noise. It sounds something like this:

'I ti tiddly y i ti ti
Yum ti tiddle i tum'

People often laugh at our doodling (in a friendly way, we hope) but respond to it all the same. It gets them moving quickly and in just the right rhythmic manner.

**Golden Rule:** Never count to the dancers. It turns them into a room full of plodders who never listen to the music, and whose brows become permanently furrowed by counting up to eight; and anyway, as we've said before, dancers don't dance on the beat (which is what you would be counting); they use the 'off beats' to carry them along.

3. You have just demonstrated the first line of the *Virginia Reel.* Now get the whole room to dance it with you and the demonstrators.

No music.

Doodle. (You will find this doodling technique particularly useful if you are working from records.)

4. Stop. With your demonstrators show the next line and a half:

'*Turn* right hand all the way round
and left hand all the way round
and two hands all the way round.'
(See glossary of figures, p. 30.)

5. Now get everybody to do it with you; doodle.

6. Then show and walk through the *Back to Back*, or '*do si do*' (half a line) – which is a bit more difficult than the other figures. (See glossary of figures, p. 34.)

Get everyone to walk it.

7. Then go through the dance as far as that with the band, or your records – and stop.

8. Then show the last two lines – the gallop, and *lead round* and arch (see glossary of figures, pages 36-8) with your 'demonstrators'. Get everybody to walk through the pattern.

Dance the last part with the music.

9. Then give the gentleman back his partner and his place – you borrowed them, remember? Bring everybody back to their starting places, and off you go with the music – no stops this time unless trouble develops.

Stay on the floor or go back on to the stage – wherever you can best keep an eye on things. Your job now is to 'call' the figures: that is, to remind the dancers, in good time, what comes next so that they have nothing to do but enjoy themselves, with your voice calling over the music, with or without a microphone.

10. Let this particular dance run four times through – once for each couple to lead it off. The easiest way to remember how many times it has gone is to fix your eye on the top couple of a set that looks reliable; when they get back to the top, you stop. It is very easy to forget to count four times through.

Either dance it again straight away if you think they'd like it (and they usually do), or let them rest for a minute before the next dance. Don't wait more than a minute before you get going on the second dance. You can have slightly longer rests later on.

So that was the technique:

With everybody on the floor show the first part of the dance.

Walk that part through and then dance it.

Show and walk the next part through. Dance it.

Put it all together and 'call' over the dancing – and if you keep cheerful, they'll respond to you.

(Even if you feel nervous – and even the most experienced callers get occasional 'stagefright' – keep it to yourself, and never, *never* get cross.)

**Golden Rule:** If things go wrong, remember it's always your fault, and not theirs. It's up to you to be patient, not them.

There are other ways of getting an evening going and there are other dances you can use, but the technique and the repertoire that follows *do* work. It's a way, in fact, of teaching without sounding like a teacher but like a friend (which is how all good teachers should sound) and it's a way of getting other people, who've never danced before, to dance in just a few minutes, with a minimum of words, and the maximum of action.

And it's real dancing you're doing – not just a party game – even though it's very simple, almost just common sense to music; you don't have to do fancy foot work to be a real dancer.

We have described all the dances that follow on the assumption that you will use, throughout the evening, this 'walking through' method. But before we describe the dances we'll give you a glossary of the common and very simple figures that occur in many of the dances. Refer back to this glossary as necessary.

### Glossary of Figures

Unless we say to the contrary, each figure is 'one line' long.

#### Forward and Back

(Or 'advance and retire' or 'in and out'.) This comes in many dances in straight line formation or in circles. Its meaning is obvious. It is usually done twice consecutively, taking up one line of music.

Beginners, particularly if they are young, lose control of this figure by taking forward steps that are too large and then finding that they are unable to do the same going backwards. Sometimes they go too far into the centre of a circle. You can help them to avoid this by your calling.

For a 'forward and back' take hands down the line at about shoulder height, and go forward for half the line. We'll use a tune to help sort it out – no counting!

**Prompt tune:** **Bobby Shaftoe's gone to sea** –
Begin to move forward

**Silver buckles on his knee**
And move back
**He'll come back and marry me**
Forward again
**Bonny Bobby Shaftoe.**
Move back.

We could say very simply 'take four steps forward and four steps back' but we don't, partly because we don't like counting, and partly because the fourth step isn't a simple one. The fourth step doesn't take the body forward like the other three, but starts to change the body's direction.

A good dancer starts off a movement in one direction strongly and finishes it in good time, ready to start in the new direction with another strong step. This is fundamental to good dancing; show it in the way you dance, without exaggeration; it's a subtle thing which most people will do quite naturally.

What this really means is that the weight of the body carries the feet along – whereas, when you count the steps you are taking, the feet tend to carry the weight of the body along.

'*In and out*' of a circle is the same as 'forward and back'. The steps are not too big; the first step is the strong one, the fourth changes the body's direction.

Of course, you don't need to say this to the dancers – just show it in the way you dance.

### Turns or Allemandes

Any turn (or allemande) takes half a line. A right-hand turn (or right allemande) is usually followed by a left allemande making a complete line of dancing.

When you're turning your partner, give her something she'll appreciate. Hold your arm up at about shoulder height, elbow slightly bent, and hold hands firmly.

DON'T give your partner a floppy hold on the end of a limp arm. DON'T give your partner a vice-like grip that comes from bulging biceps.

When you turn together, it's the relaxed weights of your two

bodies evenly distributed around a common axis that provides the fun.

Once again, as in the *forward and back*, finish off an allemande at the end of its line, ready to start the next figure with a good strong step.

**Stars – right and left-handed**

These are really allemandes for four people at once, two men and their partners. The man, as always, is on the left with his partner on his right hand side.

The two couples face.

The two ladies join right hands – just as for a right allemande – and the two men do the same with their hands above the girls' hands. Take a good firm grip. Then the weight of all four bodies, as the star starts to move around, pulling on strong, firm arms, gives pleasure to dancing the figure. It's like creating a mild feeling of centrifugal force; no bodyweight – no pleasure.

Once again, finish off a right-hand star in good time before you set off back on a left-hand star with a good strong first step.

In fact, let's mark it out to our prompt tune.

| | |
|---|---|
| **Bo** | **bby Shaftoe's gone to sea** |
| strong first step | |
| **Sil** | **ver buckles on his knee** |
| start to drop hands | start to turn back |

| | |
|---|---|
| **He'll** | **come back and marry me** |
| strong first step with left hand in place | |
| **Bo** | **nny Bobby Shaftoe** |
| start to drop hands and prepare for next figure | |

**Two Hand Turn**

Like an allemande but with both hands held at about chest height, elbows springy and slightly bent. Once again the weight of the body gives the pleasure – no flabby hands, no bulging biceps.

**Back to Back**
(or **Do-si-do,** American style).

Look at the track in the diagram:

You face your partner, go forward, right shoulder to right shoulder:

**Bobby Shaftoe's**

Keep going round, behind your partner, without turning,

**Gone to Sea**

and still without turning, move backwards into place, down the other side (left shoulders passing, this time)

**Silver buckles on his knee**

Sometimes this do-si-do, with right shoulder first, is followed by a do-si-do with left shoulder – the other way round in fact. These two together would take a whole line.

**Promenade**

This can fill any length of music you need to get from place to place. In most dances it fills a whole line.

It's up to the man to lead: both face forward, side by side; take your partner's right hand in your right hand and the left in your left, arms crossing in front – like a skating hold. For most 'control' the hands should be held at about chest height.

Promenading is usually done in what is called 'ballroom direction'; that is to say, counter clockwise.

We know of no reason for it being in this particular direction. It's just a rule of the road so that dancers don't collide.

### Down and Back
### Lead Around

Both of these take a line each, and we have put them together because they often follow one another.

There are plenty of dances (three in this book) in which the dancers are in facing lines of four or five couples. The last figure of these dances is usually the lead (or gallop) *Down and back* and *Lead around.*

The top couple (usually the one nearest the band or the M.C.) starts it off.

*Down and back:* The top man faces his partner and they take hands straight across or 'waltz hold'.

They slip or gallop step (a sidestep which will be familiar to most) down to the bottom of the set (this takes half the line),

and then back to place, for the other half of the line; they then drop hands.

*Lead around* (sometimes called 'cast off'): The top man goes out to his left, and the top lady goes out to her right. The other men follow the leading man around their side, the other ladies following their lady around the ladies' side. They lead down towards the bottom of the set.

The first couple, when they meet at the bottom, give their two hands across again and raise their arms to make an arch.

The other couples meet their partners and go under the arch and back into the set; the original second couple is now at the top of the set while the original top couple remains at the bottom.

There is only one line for this, so don't set off in a route march around the hall before you make the arch.

**Bo** **bby Shaftoe's bright and fair**
top couple turn out
and lead around
**Combing down his golden** **hair**
meet and make the
arch about now

If anyone gets back early and is stuck, with music left over, they can always swing with their partner until the line ends.

### Circling

This explains itself. It can be for two, four, eight couples, or the entire company. Join hands, the arms nearly at shoulder height, elbows slightly bent and 'springy', forming a circle.

Circles can go on for as long as you like or to the left for a line and to the right for a line or, to the left for half a line and to the right for half a line.

### Swing Partners

Not easy to write down. It's one of those things that you need to see – but we'll try.

*Position*: Stand side by side with your partner. She's facing one way and you the other, but you have her a little to your right, so that your knees don't knock together. Take up what is called 'ballroom hold' – sometimes called 'waltz hold':

*Men* – Take your partner's right hand in your left and extend, till both arms are nearly straight (elbows bent a little) and pretty well horizontal. Put your right arm round your partner, your hand between her shoulder blades (it's that right hand that really controls the swing). Lift your right elbow up until your forearm is horizontal.

*Girls* – Rest your left hand on your partner's right shoulder.

You're now going to turn or swing each other.

*The easiest way* to get the feeling of the swing is just to *walk* round, with ballroom hold, on the spot. You get quite a lot of feeling of spin that way, and it's easier for beginners than the more accomplished pivot swing.

*The pivot swing* means that with ballroom hold you 'push' yourselves round and around on the spot.

The left foot does the pushing, and the right foot acts as the pivot. It's rather like pushing an old-fashioned child's scooter around.

The feet don't move a great deal, even when you get a good strong spin going.

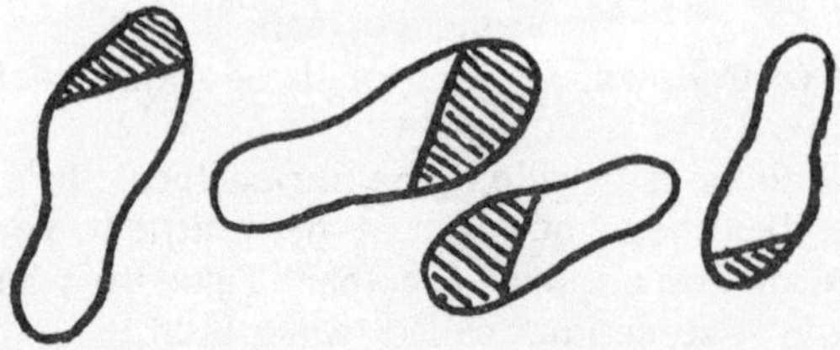

The ‘push’ from the left foot hits the off-beat of the phrase. The drop onto the pivotting right foot hits the beat itself.

Like this:

| | | | | | | | |
|---|---|---|---|---|---|---|---|
| and | one | and | two | and | three | and | four |
| left | right | left | right | left | right | left | right. |

Even though the right foot is the pivot it isn’t nailed to the floor, but just clears the floor slightly, during the push of the left foot.

By all means use a pivot swing with experienced dancers. But the walking swing is quite fun enough for inexperienced dancers, and much easier to learn.

**Balance:** This is a sort of ‘greeting’ figure, often preceding a swing. It may be ‘balance once’ (on each foot) or ‘twice’ (on each foot).

Step on the left and swing the right foot across in front, hopping a second time on the left foot.

Step on the right foot and swing the left foot across in front, hopping gently on the right foot a second time.

Now for the dances. Always refer back to the glossary for the common figures (terms described in the glossary are printed in italics) – new figures we’ll describe as we go along.

We’ll also talk about the technique of putting each dance over, although of course you will need to adapt the technique to suit the circumstances. The section on Planning a Programme in Chapter 6 will help you with the basic principles of when to do which dance.

### 1. The Big Set and Progressive Big Set

This is American, from the Appalachian Mountains, where the British settled two hundred years ago.

You can use any length of tune you like, traditionally a reel but a jig would do just as well.

This is a good dance to start with. It's very simple and it hasn't got a set pattern of figures so you can vary what you do to suit the occasion. It's just a big circle dance of splendid simplicity, for as many to join in as want to.

You can begin in a big circle with everybody facing the centre, the men having their partners on their right; or you can lead a *promenade* round the room with your partner, with everybody joining on behind in a sort of crocodile two by two (but make sure you know the people just well enough to be reasonably sure that they *will* join on behind – or there may be just you two and the vicar and his wife!).

Let's say you start off in one big circle facing the centre. Here's a suggested sequence.

| | |
|---|---|
| *1st line* | All *circle* left (for the whole line) |
| *2nd line* | All *circle* right |
| *3rd line* | All *swing* your partners |
| *4th line* | All *promenade* around, facing in at the end ready for the first line again. |

**Suggested Teaching**

1. Get the circle made up.
2. You can dance the first two lines straight away if you are dancing in with the set yourself. Stop.
3. Show and dance the swing } If you have not done these previously during the evening
4. Show and dance the promenade }
5. Now dance it all through for as long as it keeps people happy.

If all goes well, you can introduce some variations on this. Stop and introduce new figures by showing and walking if necessary, but don't bore your dancers by stopping too frequently. Remember they want to dance!

Now, here follow some figures for which the dancers need to be in two circles, one inside the other; the men on the inside, facing their partners on the outside – just as though they were promenading and have suddenly turned to face their partners. This is the traditional Big Set.

| | |
|---|---|
| *1st line* | all *allemande* right (with partners) |
| | all *allemande* left ,, ,, |
| *2nd line* | all *do si do* right shoulder |
| | all *do si do* left shoulder |
| *3rd line* | all *swing* partners |
| *4th line* | all *promenade* |

All these movements can be kept in sequence or, if you are confident of your dancers (and yourself), you can put them together by random 'calling' as you go. You can be outside the set or dancing in it yourself as you call. But you must call in good time – about half-way through the previous line – and in a good strong voice.

**Progressive Big Set**

This is another variation in which each man moves forward to a new partner every few lines. Like this:

*1st line* *allemande* right
*allemande* left

*2nd line* *two hand turn*
*do si do* right shoulder

*3rd line* all *swing* partners

*4th line* all *promenade* but as the promenade comes to an end, the men move forward to the next girl in front for an allemande right, etc.

Big Set is traditionally used quite freely in this way and is a good way of introducing new moves to your dancers. But don't introduce too many at once. If this is the early part of the first evening you'd do well to stick to the first sequence. A simple sequence danced with success is far better than a complicated one (to them) which falls apart.

## 2. The Sicilian Circle

This is a formation rather than a dance, sometimes called the Circassian Circle. Don't be put off by the exotic names. It's a very British dance and has nothing whatever to do with Sicily.

*Four lines long – jig or reel.* Try *Bobby Shaftoe's Gone to Sea.*

*Formation* A circle made up of as many couples as wish to join in, each couple facing another couple: the idea is that you dance three figures with the first couple you face and then move on to the next couple round the room. So there are as many groups of two couples as you like in a big circle around the room. Like this:

You can dance many figures in this formation: here are three that are easy and foolproof.

*1st line* *Right and left hand stars.*

*2nd line* Cross-over.

Not in the glossary, but easy enough.

**Bobby Shaftoe's gone to sea**

The two ladies cross over and change places, passing right shoulder

**Silver Buckles on his knee**

The two men do the same

**He'll come back and marry me**
The two ladies cross back (passing right shoulder, again)
**Bonny Bobby Shaftoe**
And the two men cross back
Everybody is now back home and facing the original direction ready for the next figure.

*3rd line* *Circle to the left* (in fours) and *circle* to the right.

*4th line* *Forward and back* and *promenade* on (the Progression).
**Bobby Shaftoe bright and fair**
Take a promenade hold (see the glossary) or, if you are feeling friendly, put your arm around the girl's waist while she rests her left arm on your right shoulder.
Both couples face each other.
Go forward to meet the other couple.
**Combing down his golden hair**
and go backwards to where you started.
**He's my ain for ever mair, Bonny Bobby Shaftoe.**
Go forward again, but this time pass by the other couple (left shoulders, men) promenading on until you meet the next couple coming towards you.

Then you start again at line one with the new couple and dance the three lines with them. Then you promenade on in the original direction to the next couple around the room. Keep on until everyone has had enough, or the record runs out.

**Suggested Teaching**

1. Get the sets made up. An easy way to get into this formation is first to make a big circle around the room with everyone facing inward and then make every two couples join hands in a circle of four. Make sure the couples are then facing round the room, and not into the centre.
2. Show and walk the first line.
   Dance the first line.
3. Show and walk the second line.

Dance the second line.

4. Then the third line.
5. Dance all three lines before walking the fourth line. Don't introduce the progression until you are all quite ready. In fact, don't hesitate to dance those three lines through again if your dancers still haven't got the hang of it – before you introduce line four. People often find it unexpectedly difficult and although it may seem simple to you who have worked it all out carefully beforehand, you will be surprised how easily things go wrong. So – be patient and don't hustle them.
6. Show, walk and dance the progression.

Now you're back to where you started and ready to begin. 'Call' for three or four times.

*Snags* The cross-over is quicker than people expect.

For some odd reason people are often reluctant to progress straight forward – they'll turn vaguely back the way they came, if you don't watch it.

*Variation for fun* Scatter the groups of four everywhere round the room and not just in a big circle. When they dance the last line – the progression – they have to hunt around for another couple. It all helps to liven up the atmosphere.

## 3. The Virginia Reel

An American version of a common British dance. Everybody's got their own version – Scots, Irish, English. Perhaps even the Welsh had one, once.

This is another good starter.

The version here is slightly simplified. (All the figures are in the glossary, page 29ff.)

*Five lines long – jig or reel*

This is a five line dance and it has, of course, five figures to match the five lines. If you haven't a five line tune then the tune won't repeat when the dance does, but this doesn't really matter.

*Formation* Men in one line facing their partners who are in the other line. Only four couples is best for beginners.

| | | |
|---|---|---|
| *1st line* | The lines go *forward and back* twice. | |
| *2nd line* | All | *allemande right* with partners |
| | ,, | *allemande left* ,, ,, |
| *3rd line* | ,, | *two hands turn* ,, ,, |
| | ,, | *do-si-do* (right shoulders) |

*4th line* The top couple *down and back.*
*5th line* All *lead around* and under the arch.

Dance it four times through or until the record stops.

**Suggested Teaching**

1. Get your sets made up.
2. Show, walk and dance the first line.
3. Then show and walk the second and third lines as far as the two hand turn.
4. Dance up to there, and stop.
5. Show and walk the do-si-do.
6. Dance the whole of the first three lines.
7. Show lines four and five.
8. Back to the beginning and off you go. You 'call'.

*Don't forget*

'Show' means that you and your 'demonstrators' walk the figure through while the rest watch.

'Walk' means everybody doing slowly what you have just been showing.

'Dance' means what it says – moving up to tempo, either to your doodling or to the music.

*Snags* '*Back to back*' (do-si-do) – doesn't explain itself. If you say 'back to back' your dancers will just stand back to back!

*Lead Round* – don't let them set off right to the bottom of the hall before they make the arch.

## 4. The Blaydon Races

This is a kind of Big Set dance. Use the tune of Blaydon Races, if the band can play it. Otherwise any four line tune will do. Here is *Blaydon Races*.

*Four lines long – jig*

*Formation* A big circle with everyone facing the middle of the hall, men with their partners on their right.

*1st line* *In and out* twice.

*2nd line* Turn and face partner and take ballroom hold and chassis or slide (i.e. the man steps to the left and closes his right foot to his left in a sliding manner.

The lady does the opposite) two steps towards the centre and two steps out again. Repeat that.

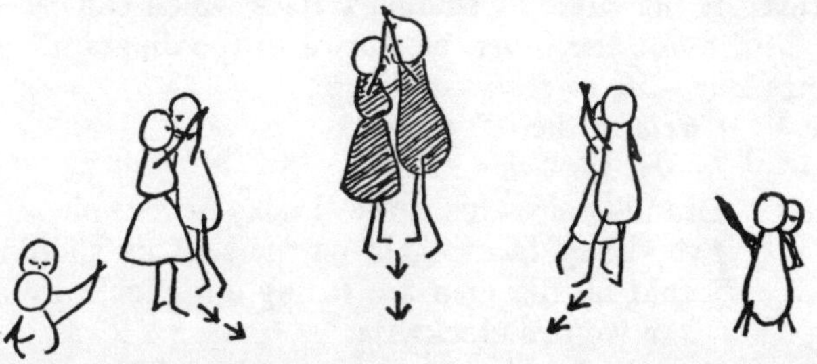

*3rd line* All *promenade*. (Remember this is always in an anti-clockwise direction.)

*Progress* It's usual, at the end of the third line for the men to move forward and swing the next girl (not the partner they have just been dancing with) for the fourth line. Then this girl becomes their partner for the next three lines of the dance.

*4th line* All *swing* partners.

**Suggested Teaching**

1. Get the circle made up.
2. Dance the circle.
3. Show and dance the chassis.
4. Dance the promenade and swing.
5. Leave the progression until you have danced the dance a few times.

## 5. Lucky Seven

Easy and fun.

*Formation* A big circle or smaller circles which can be one inside the other, as shown in the diagram.

*Four lines long – Jig or reel, usually jig.*

*1st line* *Circle* to the left only.

*2nd line* *In and out* twice.

*3rd line* Grand chain: this is the 'Lucky Seven' bit.

Everybody faces their partners. This should mean that all the men are facing anti-clockwise and all the women clockwise.

Everybody takes their partner's right hand and says 'ONE' (the louder the better). Pass partners by and take the next person by the left hand: 'TWO'!

Right hand to the next: 'THREE'.
Left hand to the next: 'FOUR'.
Right hand to the next: 'FIVE'.
Left hand to the next: 'SIX'.
On to the next, 'SEVEN', and this one you

*4th line* *swing* – she (or he!) is 'lucky seven'. At the end of the swing, men put their partners on their right hand side as they face the middle to remake the circle.

**Suggested Teaching**

1. Get your circle made up and 'borrow' a place (or if there are not too many dancers on the floor to keep an eye on, take a partner and have a dance yourself).
2. Dance lines one and two straight off – you're in the set so they will take their cue from you. Stop.
3. NOW, take your time! First make sure that when everybody is facing their partner the men are all facing anti-clockwise and the women the opposite way. You need only one person facing the wrong way to throw the whole lot! Go through line three slowly and steadily. Get them to shout the numbers if you can – they'll enjoy it and it helps a lot. You might be lucky and get everybody to 'lucky seven' first time. If not, have a good laugh and send everybody back to where they started and have another try. But keep cheerful.
   If the first walk-through is successful, don't go back to places but walk it again, starting with the new partners.
4. Line four is easy now, for they will have watched what you have done when you have reached 'lucky seven'.

*Snags* It needs only one bewildered dancer going the wrong way in the chain to throw everybody he meets into chaos. This is often because the men do not have their partners on their right hand side when they start to chain and both go off in the wrong direction. It is sometimes because someone does an *allemande* instead of chaining past.

So, keep your eye open for what is known in the trade as the 'riderless horse' – the man or woman who, if they can go wrong, will. It's not their fault, so don't get cross, but stand near and help them as much as you can – otherwise the whole of the field might come crashing down around them!

Just hope that you don't get too many 'riderless horses'. If you do, then work more slowly. Remember the golden rule: 'It's always your fault – never theirs'.

## 6. Spanish Waltz

A popular waltz-time dance, especially in the North of England. There's nothing Spanish about it – it is sometimes called the *Circle Waltz* or the *Family Waltz.* It's particularly useful when you have a number of older dancers who like an old-fashioned waltz – because that's what it is.

*Formation* A big circle or, if you prefer, smaller circles.

*Four lines – Old-fashioned waltz.*

For this one we'll use a prompt tune – *My Bonny lies over the ocean.* Most people will know that.

Of course, any waltz, traditional or popular, will do, provided it is the usual four lines (thirty-two bars) long. *I belong to Glasgow, When Irish eyes are smiling, Westering Home, The Old Bull and Bush* – these are just a few that any pub pianist will know.

*1st line* Take hands in the circle and waltz, one step in, and one step out.

**My Bonny lies over the**

In Out

Each man takes the girl on his *left* (not his partner) and passes her across in front of him into his partner's place. (The lady faces him as she passes.)

| | |
|---|---|
| **Ocean** | **(pom pom)** |
| girl across | arrived in new place |

Now the girls have all moved round the circle one place, while the men are still where they started.

Repeat this with the new left-hand girl.

| | | | |
|---|---|---|---|
| **My Bonny lies** | **over the** | **sea** | **(pom pom)** |
| In | out | new girl across | arrived |

*2nd line* This is a repeat of line one, giving the girls two more places to move on. At the end of this line, the men will have passed four girls across in front of them.

| | | | |
|---|---|---|---|
| **My Bonny lies** | **over the** | **ocean** | **(pom pom)** |
| In | out | girl across | arrived |

| | | | |
|---|---|---|---|
| **Oh bring back my** | **bonny** | **to me (pom** | **pom)** |
| In | out | girl across | arrived |

This fourth girl is the man's new partner and he faces her and takes both her hands for the next line.

*3rd line* This is rather like the *Veleta*.

A 'waltz balance': the man steps on to the left foot and at the same time swings the right leg across in front of the left leg. Then he steps on to the right foot and swings the left leg across in front. (Ladies do the opposite.)

Spin around individually, turning first towards the middle, taking two waltz steps as you turn completely round to face your partner again and take hands.

| **Bring** | **back** | **bring** | **back** |
|---|---|---|---|
| men step left | step right | spin and | turn in |

(ladies, the opposite)

Then repeat – this time going the opposite way.

Men step right; swing left leg. Step left; swing right leg and spin outwards, this time, finishing to face partner again. (Ladies do the opposite.)

| | | | | |
|---|---|---|---|---|
| **Oh** | **bring** | **back** | **my** | **bonny** |
| | step | | | step |
| | right | | | left |
| **to** | **me** | **to** | **me** | |
| | spin and turn out. | | | |

*4th line* Take ballroom hold and slide or 'chassis' two steps towards the centre and two steps out, and waltz your partner around the circle for half the line. Finish with the lady on the right of the man, facing the centre ready to take hands and begin again.

| | | | | |
|---|---|---|---|---|
| **Bring** | **back** | **bring** | **back** | **Oh bring back** |
| Slide in | in | out | out | waltz around |
| **my bonny to** | | | | **me** |
| and finish in circle | | | | now |

**Suggested Teaching**

1. Get your circle made up. You should join in this one, with either your own partner or a 'borrowed' one.
2. SLOWLY walk and dance the first two lines, sending everybody back to their places each time it looks like breaking up.
3. Show and dance the third line.
4. Show and dance the fourth line. This is the easiest line but the men must remember to put their new girl on their right when they have finished the waltzing.

*Snags*

1. This dance is not much fun if they don't like waltzing (teenagers often don't!).
2. It becomes a difficult dance if you don't show it slowly.
3. Some men will insist upon putting their partners on the wrong side at the end of the waltz or even waltzing out of the set, altogether.
   Keep your eyes open.
   Stop and start again, if necessary.

## 7. The 'Oxo' Reel

*Formation* A longways set of six couples as for *Virginia Reel* (it is important that there are six couples).

*Four lines long – Reel* (preferably).

*1st line* Everybody dances *forward and back*, and then *do-si-do* with partners.

*2nd line* The same (the do-si-do can be right shoulders in the first line and left shoulders in the second line, if you want to vary it a little).

*3rd line* The 'Oxo' bit: The first two couples make a circle and *circle* left and right.

The middle two couples dance a *right* and *left hand star*.

The bottom two couples *circle*, the same as the first two couples.

*4th line* The first couple swings through the set to the bottom place, where they continue swinging. The other couples swing as soon as they have passed them.

**Teaching**

1. Get the sets made up (check that each set has six couples).
2. Show and dance first and second lines.
3. Show line 3 and dance it.
4. Show line 4 and dance the whole dance.

(Adjust your teaching as necessary if you have already danced some of the figures earlier).

*Snags*

1. The second time through, and subsequently, everybody has something different to do in the 'OXO' bit, but this is the 'laugh' in this dance.
2. Prompt the other couples to swing as soon as each new couple passes them on their way down the set.

## 8. The Waves of Tory

A simplified version of the Irish long set dance. (It begins like the *Virginia Reel.*)

*Formation* Two lines with the men facing their partners, as in *Virginia Reel.* It is essential to have five couples.

*Six lines long – jig.*

(You could use a record with a normal four line tune; it would mean that you would get three times through the tune for twice through the dance.)

| Tune | | Dance |
|---|---|---|
| 3 x 4 lines = 12 lines | : | 2 x 6 lines = 12 lines |

Similarly the band could play a four-line tune or, if they are experienced enough not to lose count, a six-line set up like this:

2 A's
2 B's
1 A
1 B

*1st line* All *forward and back* then forward again to cross over. (The men make an arch with their joined hands and the girls duck under.) Everybody is then in their partner's place and turns to face their partner again.

*2nd line* The same as the first line with everybody crossing back to their original place.

*3rd line* The first couple *down and back.*

*4th line* The first couple *lead around* and make an arch at the bottom of the set. The others follow and go round and under the arch until they are back in their original places, with the first couple still at the bottom.

Everybody faces down toward the bottom couple who break their arch and face up, towards the the others. Then comes 'the Waves'.

*5th and 6th lines* The 'Waves'. The Americans describe this as a 'dip and dive' movement, perhaps it would be better described as an 'arch and dive' movement since each couple does just that, up and down the set, everybody 'arching and diving' until the set is back to its original order. Like this:

Everybody takes their partner's hand and the original 5th couple raises their joined hands to make an arch. The original first couple (now at the bottom) ducks under this arch, in the direction of the top of the set, and immediately makes a similar arch to go over the top of the next couple up the line (the original 4th couple), and under the next arch and so on.

Everybody starts to move as the first couple reach them. As soon as each couple reaches the bottom of the set, they turn round and follow the original first couple, under the first arch, and over the next couple and so on; 'diving and arching', in fact.

When each couple reaches the top of the set it turns round and dives under the arch (everybody still moving) and works its way back to its original place.

That's a lot of words which make a reasonably easy figure sound very difficult, but just remember three things:

1. Each couple moves *as soon* as the first couple reaches them and they keep moving until they are back where they started the 'waves'.
2. It's always dive and arch, or arch and dive (depending which you did first) until you are back again.
3. When you are at either end of the set, you turn around and come back in – *diving* (always).

It should not be too difficult for everybody to get the idea of this from your demonstration – it is certainly a lot easier to demonstrate than to describe in words.

When everyone has moved up and down the set and back to where they started the 'waves', the dance begins again with a new first couple.

**Suggested Teaching**

1. Get your sets made up – (Remember it MUST be five couples).
2. The first two lines are easy and can be danced through to doodling straight away.
3. Walk and dance the *down and up, lead round and arch*, although if you have used this earlier, you might be able to dance this through straight away as well.
4. Stop. Now, very slowly show the waves figure with your 'demonstration set'.

   Dance it to doodling with your demonstration set.

   Walk it through with everybody.

   Walk it again.

   Dance it to doodling.

   Dance it again, if necessary (and if it *is* necessary, it will still be an enjoyable repetition).
5. Come back to starting places and dance it through once. Now use your judgement. You might need to stop after the first time through for a quick sort out, or you might be able to go straight on.

   There's a new couple the next time to lead the 'waves' figure. If everyone has been 'stretched' the first time through, you might like to walk the second time through as well.

*Snags* – obvious!

1. The 'waves' is quick moving and needs the leading couple to be lively and quick off the mark. This is another figure where one couple who gets lost can wreck the whole dance – not that that isn't good fun at times, but you ought to be ready to give help where needed.
2. Emphasize, and emphasize again, that when each couple turns round to come into the set again, they *dive* first.
3. Emphasize that everyone moves as soon as the first couple reaches them.
4. Don't take too long making the arch each time.

### 9. Circassian Circle

(Sometimes called **The Flirtation**)

A very simple circle dance, popular everywhere and often used as an easy dance to finish the evening. (It is really the *second figure* of the Circassian Circle but nobody calls it that, these days.)

*Formation* A big circle, with as many couples as wish to join in.

*Four lines long – Reel or jig* and often danced to its own tune, called *Good Humour*.

*1st line* All *in and out* twice.

*2nd line* The girls only *in and out*. (Often they clap on the fourth beat.)

The men only *in and out* (clap on the fourth beat.)

*3rd line* All swing partners.

*4th line* All promenade in the big circle round the room.

**Suggested Teaching**

1. Get the dancers into place.
2. Walk it, or dance it straight away.

*Snags* None really, except that for some odd reason (perhaps because of a built-in folk memory of 'The Gay Gordons') people sometimes turn round half-way through the promenade and try to come back the other way. If everyone starts to pile up in a heap, you know that it's happened!

When you have danced a few turns and it is all going smoothly, stop and introduce:

**The Flirtation**

At the end of the second line the man returns to swing, not his partner, but the girl on his left. She becomes his new partner and he promenades her.

If it is the last dance of the evening, make sure that the men find their original partners the last time through the dance (call this just as the men go forward).

Sometimes there are more men than women at a dance, or vice versa. Here are two dances, *Three Meet* and *Red River Valley*, for one man with two partners or one lady with two partners. They use up the surplus very conveniently. Both are in the formation of the *Sicilian Circle* (*page 44*).

There are a number of these 'six-handed' dances – perhaps Scotland's *Dashing White Sergeant* is the most famous. Of the two described here, *Three Meet* is from England, *Red River Valley* probably from the United States.

Let's say that there are more ladies than men; if it's the other way round, make the obvious adjustments.

## 10. Three Meet

*Formation* As for *Sicilian Circle*, but in threes, facing each other, in a circle round the room. The man is in the middle of the three with a lady on each side. An easy way to make up the sets is to start with the threes facing round the room the same way – three behind three – and then ask every alternate three to turn around to face the three behind them to make three facing three.

Check that everyone has three to face *before* starting.

*Four lines long – jig or reel – usually a jig.*

*1st line* The threes link arms and go *forward and back* to

meet each other and retire (half a line). Then each three dances out together to the right, passing left shoulders with the opposite three and, at the same time, swivelling round to take up the opposite place.

*2nd line* This is a repeat of the first line, getting everybody back to where they started.

*3rd line* All six join hands and *circle* half the line to the left and to the right for the other half line.

*4th line* The progression. The six split up into their threes again, making two circles, and begin circling to the left and, at the same time, moving on past the three with whom they've just been dancing – out to the right, once again.

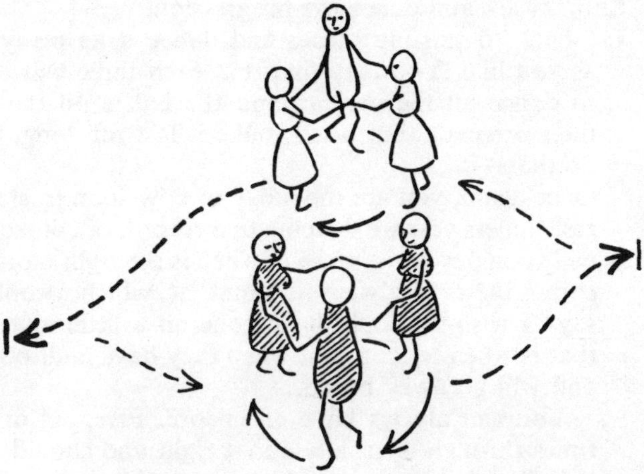

They carry on circling to the end of the line. Then the two ladies let go hands and the lines of three open up, link arms and face a new three, ready to start again.

**Suggested Teaching**

1. Get sets made up.
2. Show and walk and dance line 1.
3. Walk and dance line 2.
4. Walk and dance line 3.
5. If you think it necessary, dance through as far as there with the music before introducing the fourth line. Only you will know whether Stage 5 is necessary. Perhaps everybody's got very noisy – or has enjoyed too much wine, or both! Perhaps you have more than your fair share of 'disorientated' customers. You're not running an assault course – the pleasure comes from the music and the sociability. There is no real pleasure for the dancers to have to think hard to remember what comes next.

**Golden Rule:** It's very difficult to be too easy.

6. Show, walk and dance the progression.
7. Go back to starting places and dance it as many times as you like. You may find that each three will be able to dance all the way around the hall until they meet their originals (but don't make it last too long, just to do that!)

   Once again, you are the judge of how soon to stop and rest (unless you are dancing to a record, of course). You will soon develop a sense of when is the right moment to stop – there is always a point at which people will say, 'I wish we could have gone on a little more', and that is when to stop, not when they have had too much and will go away bored.

   You can always have an encore. Five, six or seven times through is usually about right and should ensure that healthy applause which means that they want it again.

*Note:* We don't always show, walk and dance. Sometimes you can walk the whole company through a figure without 'showing' first. Sometimes you can even dance straight away. You must be the judge, once again, according to the circumstances. People and circumstances are never the same twice: *a good M.C. is always sensitive to what to do on any particular occasion.*

*Snags*

1. Having swivelled round in line 1, occasionally someone wants to swivel again in line 4. Make sure everyone finishes facing in the right direction.
2. Emphasize that the gentlemen never let go of the girls' hands in this dance.

## 11. Red River Valley

Vaguely American, though probably somebody just made up a sequence of figures to a good tune.

*Special Tune* The well-known traditional song played as a brisk reel. Unlike most country-dance tunes it is played as one 'A' music and one 'B' music all the way through. (This is explained in the music chapter.) We have called it six lines long, just for clarity.

*Formation* A *Sicilian Circle* for three facing three (see *Three Meet*). Again we have described this using two women with each man. Of course, it can be the other way round.

This is a little more difficult than *Three Meet*. Keep it for the second half of the evening when everyone has 'got going', or keep it for a second session. It is more difficult because it starts with a progression and the figures follow each other quicker than you would think and there are two more progressions before the dance repeats itself.

This is an American 'singing call' dance. That is to say the figures fit the words of a descriptive song set to a well-known tune.

There are lots of these singing dances, many of them being danced as square dances. You will find some more, later in the book.

To begin with, here are the words which fit the tune and describe the dance.

*1st line* 'Well you pass right on down the valley
And you circle to the left and to the right

*2nd line* Then you swing with that girl in the valley
And you swing with your Red River girl.
*3rd line* Now you pass right on down the valley
And you circle to the left and to the right
*4th line* The ladies make a star in the middle
And the gents do-si-do, so polite;
*5th line* And you pass right on down the valley
And you circle to the left and to the right
*6th line* And you lose your girl in the valley
And you lose your Red River Girl'.

*1st line* The threes link arms and pass by the three they are facing (out to the right, with left shoulders passing) to face the next three.
The two lines of three join hands to make a circle of six. *Circle* to the left and back again.
(This is a very short circle left and right since it only has a quarter line for each direction.)

*2nd line* The man swings the lady on his right (or does a *two-hand turn*) and then he swings the lady on his left (or *two-hand turn*).

*3rd line* The same as 1st line – passing on to the next three around the room. *Circle* left and right (short).

*4th line* The four ladies make a *right hand* star and turn it once around (no left-hand star) and then they fall back to their places beside their man.
Then the two gents *do-si-do* with each other.

*5th line* The same as the 1st line – passing on to face yet another three. *Circle* left and right.

*6th line* The two right-hand ladies cross over diagonally to stand beside the opposite man and then the two left hand ladies cross over similarly.
As the song has said, this is where 'you lose your girl' for each man now has two new partners, one on either side, and the dance begins again with the girls going along with their new man.

**Suggested Teaching**

1. Get the sets made up.
   (See *Three Meet* on the best way to go about this.)
2. Show, walk and dance lines one and two. Point out the shortness of the circle left and circle right.
3. Show, walk and dance lines three and four. Point out that there is no left-hand star.
4. Show, walk and dance lines five and six.
5. If you think it necessary, go back to the beginning and 'doodle' it right through before you start the music.
6. Start the music and off they go. Sing the words as you go. You will find that the dancers will quickly pick up the words and sing along with you.

*Snags*

1. The short circle left and right.
2. No left hand star in line four.
3. The left hand ladies tend to cross over much too early and be left standing with their new partners waiting for the the music to catch up.
4. If you have done *Three Meet* previously, you will have to watch that no man swings his three around after the pass on.

## SQUARE DANCES

There are hundreds of square dances (four couples in a 'box, as in the *Lancers* or the *Eightsome Reel*), some of them very complicated and fast moving. The very simplest and the most enjoyable for the beginner are the 'singing' squares from America. A singing square is one that has a set sequence of figures that fit to a song, usually a popular song, the tune of which everyone is likely to know.

Here is the formation – a square or box. In square dancing, folk style, the couples are numbered round as shown.

You will see that if everyone takes hands in this formation they are actually in a circle. This is the easiest way to make up the sets – by joining hands in circles of eight (four couples) and then each man letting go of the lady on his left and each couple 'squaring' the set. One couple stands with their backs to the band (couple number one), one couple faces them (couple number three) and a couple on each side faces each other (couples two and four).

Here is an American square dance.

## 12. Buffalo Girls

*Formation* – Square set.
*Four lines long* – Any solid *reel or march* tune that hasn't too many notes in it. There is a tune called *Buffalo Girls* and we give the words to fit this tune. If you use another tune, adapt the words to fit.

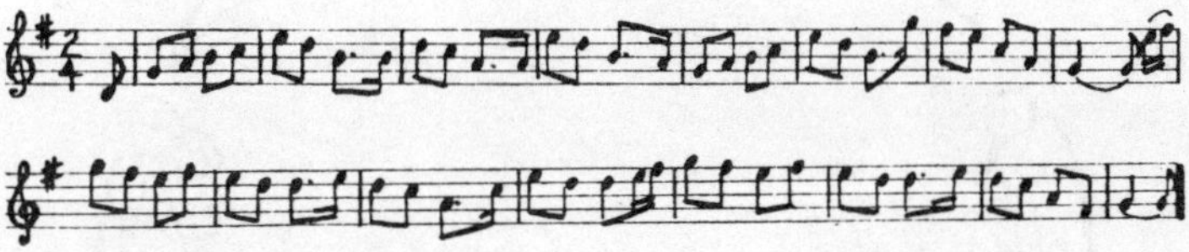

To begin with, here are the words that fit the tune, and describe the dance. You can sing this while they dance, if you like.

*The Song*

*1st line* 'First Buffalo girl go round the outside, round the outside, round the outside,
First Buffalo girl go round the outside and back home to her partner.

*2nd line* Do-si-do your partners all, partners all, your corners all,
Do-si-do your corners all and then you swing your partner.

*3rd line* You swing your partner round and round,
you swing her up you swing her down,
Swing your partner off the ground and then you promenade her.

*4th line* Promenade your partners all, your partners all, your partners all, promenade her round the hall, you promenade your partner.'

*The Dance*

*1st line* The first lady (the one with her back to the band) sets off around the outside of the set, clockwise all the way round and back to her place.

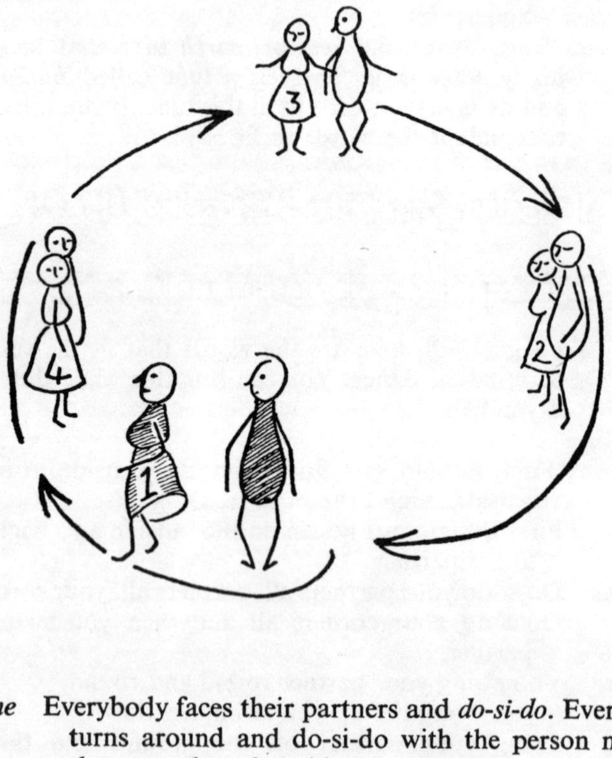


*2nd line* Everybody faces their partners and *do-si-do*. Everybody turns around and do-si-do with the person next to them, on the other side (the 'corner').

(This person next to you who is not your partner is known as 'the corner'. Thus, the first man has the fourth lady as his corner; the first lady has the second man as her corner.)

*3rd line* Everybody swing with their partner.

*4th line* All four couples promenade around (in their own square only) back to their original places in the set (in an anti-clockwise direction).

*The Second Time Through*

*1st line* Exactly the same except that there will be two girls going round (see figure overleaf).

(The third time through there will be three girls moving. And the fourth time through there will be four girls moving).

*2nd, 3rd and 4th lines* The same as the first time through the dance. Of course, you will need different words for the four different first lines, here they are:

First time through
'First Buffalo girl go round the outside, etc.'

Second time through
'Two Buffalo girls go round the outside, etc.'

Third time through
'Three Buffalo girls go round the outside, etc.'

Fourth time through
'Four Buffalo girls go round the outside, etc.'

Then if all is going well:

'First Buffalo *Gent* go round the outside . . .'
and so on for the four men.

You may find that, for anyone who has not done this sort of thing before, this dance is not quite as simple as it sounds; but with the right sort of party atmosphere and a good thump to the music it's just easy enough for them to have a great time. They'll love it!

**Suggested Teaching**

1. Get your sets made up – refer back to pp 72–3 to see the best way to do this.
2. Number the couples in each set.
   'Couple number one has their backs to the band. Wave you hand in the air, couple number one.'
   'Couple number two, you're over this side. Wave your hand, couple number two.'
   'Couple number three, you're facing the band. Give us a wave.'
   'Couple number four – hullo there!' (or invent your own corn).
3. Remind the first ladies who they are. Sometimes the girls rely on partners to do all the remembering!
4. Walk all the first ladies off on their tracks. Walk the next two lines.
5. Walk the first and second ladies off on their tracks. Walk the second lines again. Explain the rest of the dance. Don't explain the Buffalo Gents bit – that can come as a surprise. A few surprises, as long as they are simple and easy to cope with are part of your stock-in-trade. The men should start off in an anti-clockwise direction, but it's not vital. They'll sort it out for themselves.

*Snags* None. Even the riderless horses will manage this one.

*The singing* Try to sing it if you possibly can. You don't need a good voice, but it helps tremendously as a rhythmic reminder and it helps the 'spirit' of the dance along If you don't fancy it, then call out, in good time, in the usual way.

## 13. Hinky Dinky

Try this one to *Mademoiselle from Armentières.*

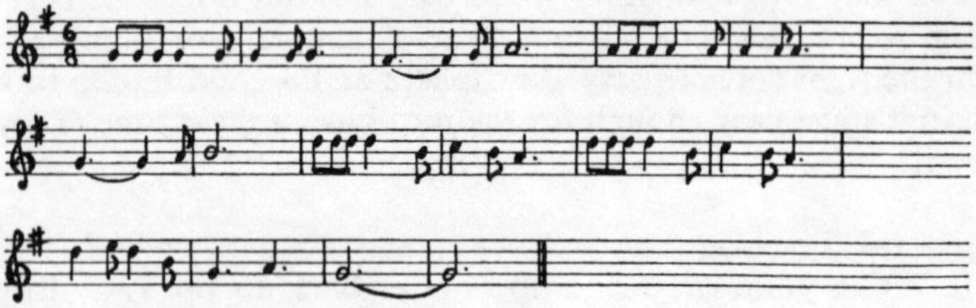

Failing that, any jig will do.
*Formation* – Square Set.
*Four lines long – Jig.*

In this dance there are head couples – the first and third; and side couples – the second and fourth.

*The Song*

*1st line* 'The two head ladies forward and back<br>
Parlez vous<br>
Forward again and back to back<br>
Parlez vous

*2nd line* Now do-si-do your partners all<br>
Then do-si-do your corners all<br>
Hinky Dinky parlez vous.

*3rd line* Now swing your partner round and round<br>
Parlez vous<br>
Swing her up and swing her down<br>
Parlez vous

*4th line* And promenade your partners all<br>
Promenade around the hall<br>
Hinky Dinky parlez vous.'

*The Dance*

*1st line* The women of the two head couples (first and third) go forward to meet each other and fall back to their places.

Then they go forward again, but this time they go back to back (*do-si-do*) in the centre.

*2nd line* Everybody *do-si-do* partners and then *do-si-do* with the corner.

*3rd line* All *swing* your partners. (If this is too long a swing – perhaps you have some older people with you who get dizzy – just put in a step or balance before the swing)

*4th line* All *promenade* round the set and back to places.

Then you repeat the figures, starting with *side* ladies dancing the first line. Then go through the whole thing again with the head men, followed by the side men, dancing the first line.

If you like you can even go on to let the head *couples* (and then the side *couples*) dance the first line.

*Additional figure* (whenever you feel like throwing it in). *Grand Chain and Promenade*

This is two lines long, but as *Mademoiselle* is usually played as a two-line tune it can fit in anywhere you like in the dance.

*1st line* All face your partners, give right hands. Pass on and give left hand to the next, then right hand to the next and so on, until, having passed your partner once, you meet her when you get home again.

*2nd line* Promenade once around, back to places.
*If you want to sing*, here are some words:
'It's right to your own, and left to the next
Parlez vous,
Yes right to your own and left to the next
Parlez vous,
Now promenade your partner round
Promenade up and promenade down,
Hinky, Dinky parlez vous.'

**Suggested Teaching**

1. Get your sets made up. Show and walk first line.
2. Show and walk the second line, then dance as far as this to the music.
3. If this is not the first square dance of the evening you can probably go straight on to the third and fourth lines – the music carries on and you call over the top of it.
4. Stop, and walk the grand chain fairly slowly, after you've been through the first four lines to music.
5. Point out that if couples *do-si-do*, they do so only with the one person opposite.

*Snags* None. Give plenty of warning when the grand chain is coming up.

## 14. Coming Round the Mountain

Another very simple sequence of figures that you can dance to the popular tune. Many other tunes will do just as well – *Yankee Doodle*, *Yellow Rose of Texas*, *Little Brown Jug*, or, if you are feeling patriotic, *The British Grenadiers*.

*Formation* – Square.

*Four lines long* – *Reel.*

*1st line* First couple *promenade* anti-clockwise around the outside of the set back to place (See Fig. A, page 83). It helps if the other couples move in a little as they do so.

*2nd line* The first couple dance a *right and left hand star* with the opposite couple (i.e. couple number three). (Fig. B).

*3rd line* Everybody *do-si-do* with partner and *swing* partner.

*4th line* All four couples *promenade* around the set (in the usual anti-clockwise direction) back to place.

The second time through the second couple will promenade and they will dance their star with the fourth couple.

The third couple lead for the third time through and star with couple number one.

The fourth couple lead the fourth time through and star with couple number two.

If you are dancing to a record that plays the tune six times

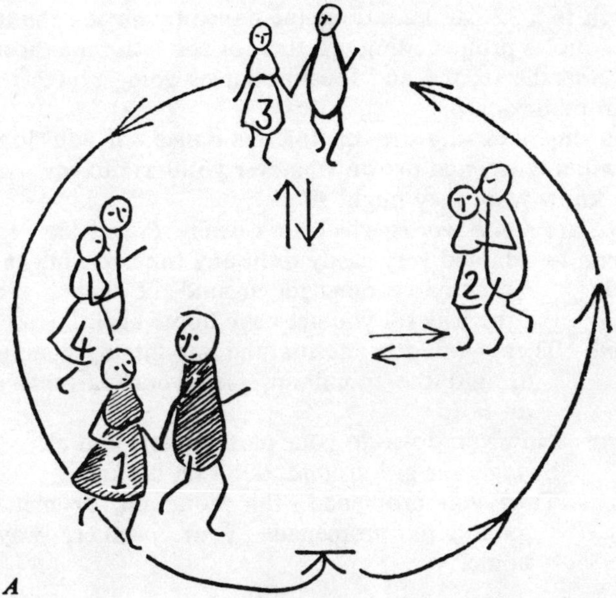


*Fig. A*

*Fig. B*

through (6 x 32 bars) continue the dance by having the first and third couples promenading together for the fifth time through the tune; and the second and fourth couples going together for the sixth time through.

You ought to sing the call for this dance – if you don't sing, they will anyway and drown whatever you have to say – and you never know what they might sing!

Here are some words which fit *Coming Round the Mountain*, they can be adapted very easily to fit any tune you might use.

*1st line* 'First couple promenade around the ring
All the way till you get back home again.

*2nd line* Then you star across the mountain, coming back around the mountain, face your partners all and do-si-do.

*3rd line* Now you do-si-do your partners one and all
Swing your girl around, don't let her fall.

*4th line* Then you promenade the mountain, promenade the mountain, promenade your partner, way back home.'

**Suggested Teaching**

1. Get your sets made up (See *Buffalo Girls*, page 73).
2. Make sure everybody knows which number couple they are.
3. Walk the whole dance through. (You shouldn't need to demonstrate more than the first line.)
4. Dance the first time through with the music; stop if necessary and walk the track for the second couple. Don't stop if all is going well for most of the sets. Those few who haven't sorted it out the first time will have done so by the second time through.

*Snags* None. Don't let your singing take your attention off the dancers. If they are lost, forget your song and 'prompt' call (i.e. talk, don't sing).

## 15. Marching Through Georgia

There are several versions to this popular marching song. This is a simple one. It derives from The Lancers.

*Formation* – Square.

*Four lines* – *March or Reel;* the dance can be fitted to many other four line tunes.

*1st line* The first couple 'separate', that is they turn their backs

on each other and set off round the outside of the set, in opposite directions, passing each other on the opposite side of the set and meeting again when they arrive back at their home place. (The man will be in his lady's place and the lady in her man's place.)

*2nd line* The first couple *do-si-do* when they arrive back home and then they swing.

At the end of the swing they finish by 'facing out' – with their backs to the circle, lady on the man's right. While they do this 'facing out', the other three couples fall in behind, in any order, and facing in the same direction. Like this:

*3rd line* The two lines separate and *lead around*, the men going to the left and the ladies to the right, following the leader. The two lines lead all the way round and back to where they started (singing the words (below) if they feel like it).

*4th line* Everybody *do-si-do* with their partner (still in line). Everybody *swings* their partner *back to their own home places.*

Then it's the second couple's turn to lead the dance and they separate, go round, do-si-do and swing. When they face out, the others fall in behind and this time everyone will be facing across the room.

Here's a call song to fit *Marching Through Georgia;* if you use another tune, adapt the words to fit.

*1st line* 'First old couple separate, go out around the ring, all the way around until you get back home again.

*2nd line* Do-si-do when you get back home
And give that girl a swing,
Turn around, you face out,
And the others fall in behind – Sing!

*3rd line* Hoorah, hoorah, we bring the jubilee,
Hoorah, hoorah, the flag to set you free.

*4th line* Now everybody do-si-do
And swing her home for me
For that's the way they do it
Down in Georgia.'

**Suggested Teaching**

1. Get the sets made up (see *Buffalo Girls*, page 73).
2. Make sure that everyone knows which number couple they are.
3. Walk the first and second lines. This should not give any difficulty if you have done plenty of *do-si-do's* earlier on.
4. Make the first couple face out and get the others to fall in behind. Point out that it doesn't matter in which order they are.
5. Walk the third line.
6. Walk the fourth line. Point out that while they are swinging they swing back to their home places in the set.
7. Explain that it's now the second couple's turn to separate, etc. Get them to 'face out'.
8. Square the set and off you go.

*Snags*

1. People are sometimes very loath to separate and let go of their partner, the one person who is giving them confidence, at the beginning of the first line and again at the third line.
2. Occasionally the leading couples start off by crossing over with each other and going the opposite way. It doesn't really matter.
3. Be a little careful with the 'facing out'. It might help to

'face' each couple in their 'out' direction before you start the music. It is turning their back on things that puts people off their stride.

Again, this is a 'singing call' and by all means sing it if you possibly can. Part of the enjoyment of this dance is the chorus line which everyone sings as they march around and if you are already singing, they will join in much more readily.

They shouldn't get lost, but if they do you can always 'prompt' call.

## 16. Cumberland Square Dance

Here are two English Square Dances.

In Cumberland, of course, they just call it the Square Dance or Square Eight. Like many other country squares it's made up of a group of quadrille figures that used to be danced separately.

We've thought a lot about whether to include this dance in a book for beginners because of the nature of the third figure, but it's such a popular and rousing dance that we've put it in.

Beware the third figure.

*Eight lines long – Jig or Reel – usually a Reel.*

The first three figures are led by the first couples (one and three), while the side couples (two and four) rest. Then the side couples repeat the figures and the heads rest. So anybody who's danced it before can go as head couple. The nervous or shy can go as side couple. To give plenty of room for the first figure we often put the sets on a diagonal, not square to the walls. (See diagram.)

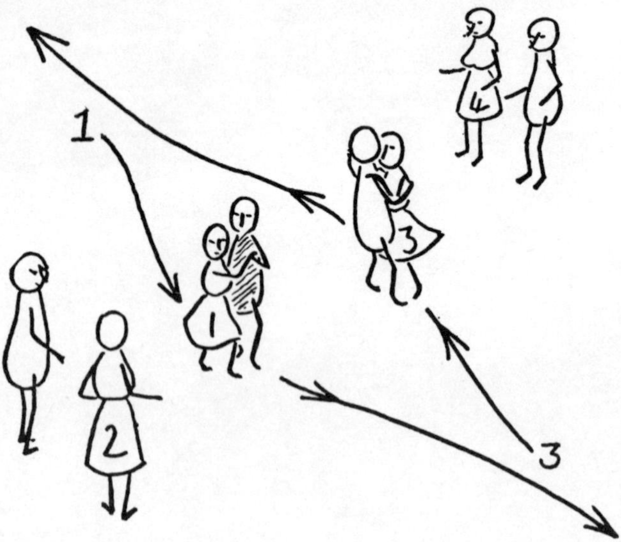

*1st line* The Gallop (or Galop if you prefer).

The two head couples take ordinary ballroom hold and slip or gallop sideways across the set. Then, without turning round, they gallop back again.

The men go back to back on the way over, the women on the way back. Don't forget it's a half line in *each* direction.

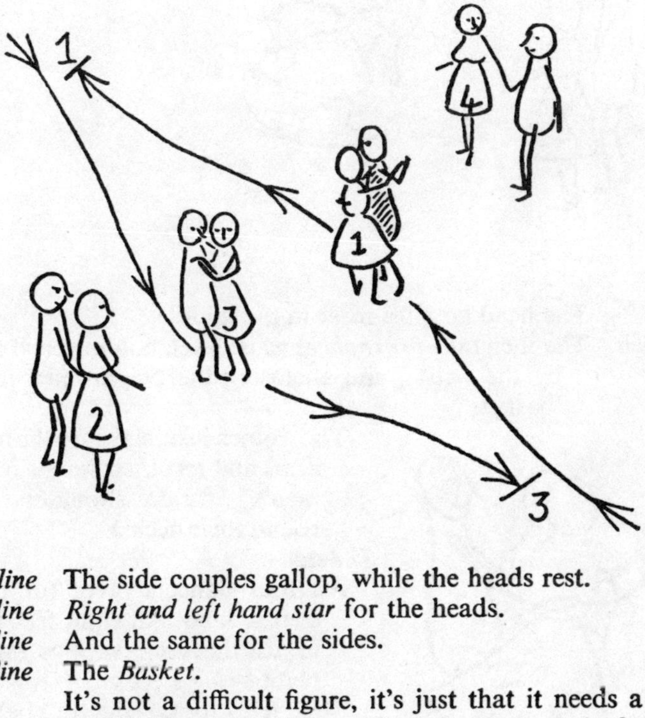


*2nd line* The side couples gallop, while the heads rest.

*3rd line* *Right and left hand star* for the heads.

*4th line* And the same for the sides.

*5th line* The *Basket*.

It's not a difficult figure, it's just that it needs a little skill to get the pleasure from it. (See overleaf.)

When badly done, it's not fun and a bit of a strain.

*The position*

The head couples meet in the middle.

The men take *firm hold* at waist level, holding each other by the wrists, and enclosing the two women in the 'baskets'.

The women just relax into the men's arms and rest their hands on the men's *nearest* shoulders (*not* round their necks).

*The step*

All four dancers pivot (or buzz) step around. All eight feet work in just the same way as far the pivot *swing* step.

The left foot, slightly behind, pushes.

The right foot, slightly in front, is the pivot.

The left foot hits the 'off' beat – the 'and'.

The right foot hits the beat – the 'one', 'two', three'.

| | | | | | | | |
|---|---|---|---|---|---|---|---|
| **and** | **one** | **and** | **two** | **and** | **three** | **and** | **four** |
| left | right | left | right | left | right | left | right |

Both feet clear the floor slightly when they are not being 'used'; in other words, the weight of the body transfers from one foot to the other, throughout the figure. The right foot is the pivot and the left foot is the power.

Try it slowly on your own and you'll find that the body rises slightly on the off beat and drops on the beat.

The step and figure are easy and relaxed, but the basket can work up quite a speed – but speed only comes with relaxed control, not strain.

All four dancers should have their heads up, looking at each other, not their feet. The bodies are over the feet, not leaning in or out. In fact the four bodies 'sit' into the eight arms like an easy chair!

Once the basket gets moving it's great fun.

*6th line* The side couples repeat the basket.

*7th line* *Big circle.*

All four couples *circle* left.

*8th line* All *promenade* home the other way.

The dance is usually danced at least twice through without stopping. Sometimes the band play a reel the first time (64 bars) and a jig the second time (64 bars).

**Suggested Teaching**

1. Either show before you get the sets up, using volunteer couples, or show with sets on the floor already. Let's assume the latter.
2. Show and dance the first two lines – easy.
3. Dance the third and fourth lines straight away if you've already included stars previously in the evening. If not (or if you think they've forgotten) show and then dance.
4. Show and walk the basket figure carefully for each pair of couples. You can even wander around and check a few 'holds' if the company is not too large. Watch par-

ticularly for the neck-grabbing ladies – they push the men's heads forward.

Then dance, etc.

5. Go straight into dancing the last two lines to your calling, unless you judge that you should show them first.
6. Now all the way through – no stops. You call the figures.

*Snags*

1. If you put your sets on the diagonal, make sure all the head couples are working in the same direction, to avoid collisions.
2. Watch out for gallopers who come back to their places after only about four slip steps.
3. The basket needs a little care to get real pleasure – not too much, of course – it isn't a dancing class (at least, it should not *appear* so).

   Watch out for:

   people leaning out,
   girls grabbing the men's necks,
   women leaning on to men who aren't gripping well and who let go, shooting the girls off at a tangent,
   any right feet getting stuck on the floor.

   Try to show it well – not easy if you're the only experienced dancer there. There may be some Old Tyme dancers about who could help out the demonstration.

   If you think the company can't manage the basket, substitute a *circle* left and right for four – a bit tame, but they don't know what they're missing.

   When they've got the hang of it, or if they've done it before, you may get another problem. Some dancers can make the baskets go so fast that, by lifting their wrists, the men can swing the ladies out horizontally. This can be dangerous – the stationary couples can receive glancing blows from passing feet, or the poor girls can be dropped on to their chins. So, in the words of the old country M.C.s, 'Kindly keep the ladies on their feet, please'.
4. It's a long *circle* to the left in line 7.

## 17 La Russe

A very popular Square Dance with an English and a Scottish version. It is not quite so easy as the others, so keep it until your dancers feel really confident – perhaps until the second visit. This version is the English one.

*Formation* – Square Set.

*Eight lines long – reel.* It also has its own tune of the same name, but any reel will do. (*Red River Valley, Buffalo Girls, Coming Round the Mountain.*)

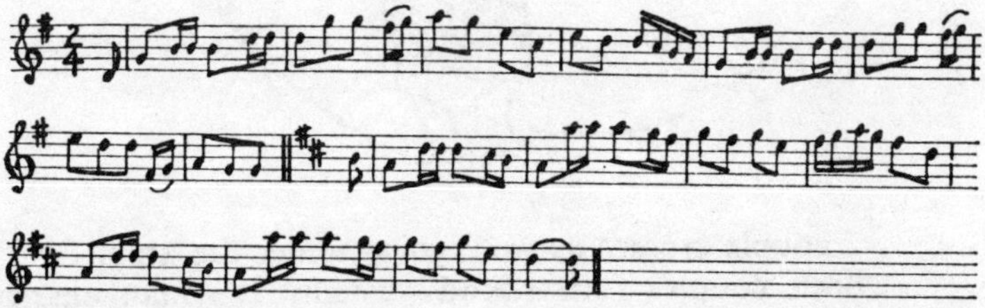

*1st line* All face your partner, and pass her by, to meet the next girl round the set. The men move in an anti-clockwise direction on the outside of the set and the girls inside. (See Fig. A overleaf.)
*Balance*, once (on each foot) to this girl, and *swing* her.

*2nd line* Leave that girl and come right back to starting places (the men outside again) to face your partner.
*Balance* to partners and *swing* partners.

*3rd line* The first couple only carries on swinging, the others clap.

*4th line* The first couple *promenades* (anti-clockwise) *inside* the set – giving a nod to each couple, if they feel like it – back to their place.

*5th line* *The arches*. The opposite couple (the third in this case) makes an arch and crosses over the set while the first

*Fig. A*

couple crosses as well, going under the arch.

Both couples turn round – usually the man changes sides with his partner *as well*, and they cross back. (See Fig. B.)

*Fig. B*

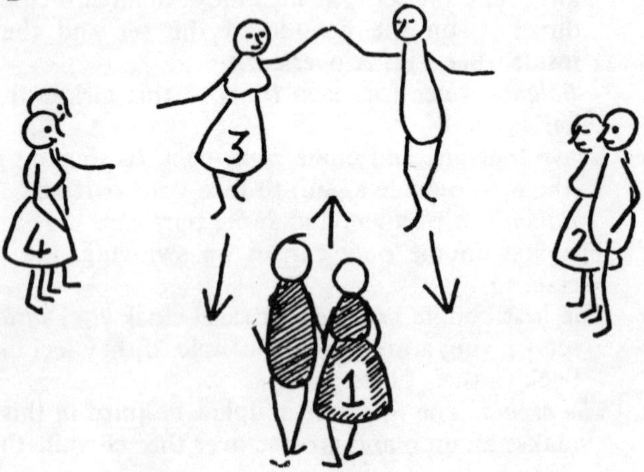

This time the *first* couple *arch* and the *third* couple *go under.*

*6th line* Repeat the 5th line – don't rush it.

*7th line* All *circle* left.

*8th line* All *promenade* home to starting places.

Then the dance starts all over again. This time the second couple dance lines 3 and 4. (Next time it will be the third, and then the fourth.)

This means that the second and fourth couples will be the next to dance lines five and six.

Dance the whole dance four times through.

**Suggested Teaching**

1. Leave this dance until the dancers are fairly experienced – the end of the evening, or the next time you come.
2. Teach the first two lines very carefully. The third and fourth are easy. Dance the first four lines and stop.
3. Walk the fifth and sixth lines carefully. Don't let them rush this part. The seventh and eighth lines are easy.
4. Stop after the first time through, and sort out the second couple's part.

*Snags* *None*, if you take it steadily, but

1. Give plenty of warning of the first figure.
2. Don't let them rush the arches figure.
3. It's a long *circle* to the left in line 7.

Chapter 5

# Organizing the dance itself

(to help you set the evening up)

We often call country dance evenings Barn Dances. You might like to run one with your club or help to run one for someone else.

**The Occasion**

Just about any occasion may be used as an excuse to hold a barn dance. The usual party occasions – New Year, Christmas, birthdays and twenty-firsts, anniversaries, weddings – are all obvious, but there are others, not so obvious, which make suitable pegs on which to hang your dance.

The Harvest Supper is very suitable and many churches hold this annual event, starting with supper and rounding off the evening with some dancing. Firework Night is also ideal. Again, if it is fine, this is a pleasant way of passing Midsummer's Eve in the garden. (But take care with all outdoor events – it is much harder to raise any 'atmosphere' out-of-doors.)

Your dance doesn't have to be a money-raiser, of course, but many are. A barn dance must be one of the cheapest ways of raising funds. Unlike many other fund-raising activities where a heavy initial outlay on equipment is needed, or a great deal of work has to be done in the preparation of entertainments, sideshows, etc., a barn dance requires nothing more than the records (which you may very well have already) or, even better, adequate musicians to provide the music for you. All you need is music and a place to dance – and the dancers, of course!

Although outlay may be minimal, a certain amount of preparation and forethought – none of it particularly arduous – is well worth the energy spent upon it if you want your dance to be a success. Let's have a look at some of the things you will need to bear in mind if you are thinking of running a dance. You may well find it useful to refer to *Raise Cash – Have Fun*, by Christine Fagg. It contains much helpful information.

**Choosing a Date**

This needs a little more thought than is at first apparent.

You will not want your dance to clash with any other function taking place nearby, or even with a national event which will have people glued to the television all the evening.

A way of finding out what is happening locally is to check with your local newspaper what happened at that particular time last year. Then you can see if the same events are taking place this year and can avoid clashing dates. Bear in mind that you might need to think about alternative dates if your hall is one that is often over-subscribed.

National events are more difficult to forecast unless they are 'annuals' such as the Cup Final, Wimbledon, etc., but most national Dailies can tell you what lies ahead for six months at least. If you are wondering why a national event could affect your church hall function, just try holding a dance when there's a Heavyweight World Championship fight on TV, and you will soon see!

**The Venue**

If you are using your garden (or the Vicar's) then there is no problem – unless you are worried about your lawn or the neighbours being disturbed. If you are looking around for a hall, however, then there are one or two things which need some thought.

Firstly, you need to consider how many people you are expecting to come. If you are going to sell two hundred tickets, then you should be thinking in terms of two hundred people being able to dance, all at one time. They probably won't, but they may.

As a rough guide, about sixty to eighty people are able to dance together on an area about the size of a badminton court but, in addition, you need to have room outside this for people to sit out between dances.

You may decide on the number you are likely to get and then look for a hall; or you may already have a hall available and have to decide how many you are able to cope with. Whichever way round it is, it is better to fill your hall so that you have *just* too many dancers. Too few can result in lack of atmosphere and be disastrous; many too many will mean that you will be unable to dance at all for people cluttering the sides of the hall. A few too many is just fine and always produces the right sort of atmosphere; it also allows the faint-hearted to rest now and again without appearing to be unsociable.

If you have a hall which you know will be too big for the expected number coming, it's always possible to close off some of the hall with home-made ranch-style fencing. (One of us took a dance on one occasion where this had been done and a pony was stabled in the non-used half of the school hall!)

More or less any kind of hall can be used. School halls are not the most atmospheric of places, but many Parent-Teacher Associations hold regular dances, full of the right spirit, in their own hall – which costs them nothing to hire.

The 'room behind the pub' often provides the right spirit, in more ways than one, and this has the advantage that it is probably licensed for music and dancing, and the neighbours are resigned to the noise. It might also be free if the dancers drink up!

If you can find a clean, empty barn with a reasonable floor, that's fine. If you are using a hall which is unfamiliar to you and someone else is responsible for the unlocking of the doors, make sure you know who it is, and where he may be found should he not be there when you arrive. Also make absolutely sure of the time at which your booking begins and ends. You may need time before the dance to make some preparations and you will certainly need some time after the dance to do some clearing up. Many a last dance of the evening has been brought to an abrupt end by the appearance of the caretaker jangling a bunch of keys – and the washing-up not even started!

Electricity arrangements also need checking. While hall lights are usually easily found, some platforms have the most complicated electrical arrangements which only an expert can understand – and the band (if you have one) might not appreciate playing in the semi-dark.

Neither will the band like a piano that is half a tone out of tune with their other instruments, so don't forget to check that.

So, you have your hall booked – what else do you need to be thinking about?

**Advertising**

You will know just how much advertising you need, or can afford. If it is just a club evening, then very little more than an announcement in the general programme is needed – although you might like to consider inviting similar clubs in the neighbourhood to come along. If it is a money-raising affair, then you must spread your net much wider and you might want to make posters, or even have some printed.

Whether you make your own or have them printed, keep to good, bold lettering and include only the important details. Don't make them too large, if you are going to ask shopkeepers to put them in their windows.

IN AID OF SCOUT FUNDS

---

**BARN DANCE**
**(Cowboy Style)**

on
SATURDAY, 3RD NOVEMBER
8.00 - 11.00 p.m.

at
THE SCOUT HUT

---

**Admission £2·50**
*(including Hot Dog Supper)*

---

| | |
|---|---|
| COME DRESSED | LEAVE GUNS AT THE DOOR |

Something like this will do. If you think your band or caller is likely to be an attraction, add their names as well.

Advertising space may also be taken in the local newspaper,

but this can prove expensive unless your return is fairly certain. You might be able to persuade your editor to run a free announcement for you in the form of a news item, particularly if you can let him have a good photograph to illustrate the item – maybe a group of cowboys making the decorations or pulling home a cart.

Local papers usually go to press about three days before they are published, so don't leave it too late to contact the editor.

### Tickets

If you want to raise money, or if finance is important, it is advisable to have tickets and to have them on sale well beforehand. If it does happen to be a wet night, people are more likely to turn out if they have already bought a ticket. In any case, many will be prepared to buy a ticket just to support your cause, if it is a worthwhile one. It is a little less depressing if, by chance, you happen to have picked the night of the England versus Brazil match if you already have most of the money in the bag!

The number of tickets sold is also a useful guide to the catering arrangements (see Refreshments, page 104).

### Special Occasions

Of course you may be holding the dance to celebrate a twenty-first birthday or a wedding, but there are also plenty of calendar dates which make suitable occasions – Guy Fawkes' Night, for instance, or Twelfth Night, St. Valentine's Eve, St. Patrick's Night and, as we mentioned before, Midsummer's Eve and Harvest Supper. If your dance is to celebrate an occasion like this, you can make the most of the theme to build up some atmosphere. Other suggestions for themes which are not dependent on the calendar are: Cowboys, Mexican, Chinese, Nautical, the Twenties, Pirates, Farm Night, Tramps' Supper – in fact, just about anything will do.

At this sort of occasion you should expect your dancers to come 'dressed' and this must be made clear on the ticket. To encourage them to come dressed appropriately, you can always make those who are not properly costumed pay for it. This could be done by extracting a 'fine' at the door or, alternatively, giving a free raffle ticket to anyone who is in costume.

If it is a fancy dress occasion, don't forget to mention it to the band – they might be prepared to dress up too. On the other hand, don't ask them to dress up if no one else is going to do so.

You don't have to wear your Sunday best to have a good time, so if it is not a fancy-dress dance and you don't want your dancers to turn up in their best clothes, put 'casual wear' on the tickets.

**Decorations**

Whatever your hall, decorations will improve its appearance. Just how elaborate they need to be will depend upon how much you are trying to disguise otherwise drab surroundings, but in any case they should be easy to put up and take down in the shortest possible time. This is particularly important if the hall has been hired just for the occasion.

This is not a job for anyone who has something else to do on the night. Preferably it should be in the hands of a small group of people who will make the decorations and put them up beforehand. They should then be free to enjoy the evening's dancing until the time comes for the decorations to be taken down again.

If the dance is to celebrate a special occasion, the decorations should fit the theme: for a 'Cowboy Dance' or Hoedown, for instance, you could use saddles, stirrups, harness, horseshoes, etc. (borrowed from the riding school), lanterns, wheels, etc. (borrowed from the Scouts), coloured blankets, coils of rope, bales of straw, etc. Just one word about straw – don't be tempted to scatter it over the floor, as odd wisps of straw lying about can make it dangerously slippery. Confine it to the stage or band corner.

For a Hallowe'en dance, you could have paper or cardboard cut-outs of witches and cats hung up and if your decorating committee is skilled enough, artificial cobwebs. Whatever your theme, the possibilities are limitless, provided your committee is given plenty of time to think about them.

Now, you've booked your hall, arranged for decorations, sold tickets, what other preparation is needed?

**Refreshments**

The refreshments can add tremendously to the success of your dance. When people are talking about your dance afterwards, they will remember the refreshments as much as the dancing and, if they have been inadequate, they will certainly say so.

The facilities available largely govern what is laid on, although it is surprising what some people can manage to prepare with only the minimum.

Even with no facilities at all, there need not be any overwhelming problem. If, say, ten interested ladies each bring one heaped plateful of sandwiches or savouries and another of small cakes, this should be sufficient for about sixty people and no-one has a lot to do at the hall beforehand.

On the other hand, with good facilities, there is no limit to what you can do, and if your dance has a theme then the refreshments too could be made to fit it.

With a cowboy dance, for instance, the menu could be 'ranch house style', with sausage and beans or beefburgers. Hot-dogs are also ideal for dancing cowboys and, if you are able to warm the rolls, all the better (and don't forget the mustard!)

On other occasions practically anything will go! Cheese and wine can be fine; in some places we have seen just a bread and cheese and onion supper served and in others we have sat down to a four-course meal, including smoked salmon! In fact, just about anything as long as it is a bit more substantial than plain biscuits and lemonade.

Whatever your refreshments, it is a good idea to include them in the price of the ticket. People are generally willing to pay more for their ticket if they see that the refreshments are included – but the refreshments must be seen to be worthwhile when they are served.

Serving the refreshments can create a problem, especially if people are asked to choose what they want. This always creates queues. A far better idea is to have plates of refreshments made up beforehand so that all people need do is pick up a plate. Paper plates are useful for this.

The easiest way of serving coffee is to take it round the hall on a trolley or on trays. The same trolley can be used for collecting the empty cups afterwards.

And, to remind you of something we said earlier, if you are having a band to play for you, don't forget to offer them some refreshments – they often do get left out, quite unintentionally, of course.

**A Bar or Not**

It is difficult to say whether a bar is a good thing or a bad thing to have at your dance. It all depends on your people and, to some extent, on where the bar is sited. Generally speaking, to have a bar in another room, away from the actual dancing is not a good thing for this tends to make people congregate at the bar when they arrive and, human nature being what it is, some of them will never leave it. If that's what they have come for, good luck to them, but it won't much help the dance. And even if you do get your new arrivals to tear themselves away from the bar, it is too good an excuse for the men to disappear now and again throughout the evening.

A bar in the same room as the dancing is much better, but of course you need plenty of space for that. Some dances, where no bar is available, allow customers to bring their own bottles. But check this is all right with the hall owners. They may not allow it.

If you are having any alcoholic drink available, you should certainly check the local licensing laws. Information about this may be obtained from The National Council of Social Service, 26 Bedford Square, London, W.C.1.

Alternatively, you might be able to persuade the local publican to run a bar for you (and if he is generous enough, he may possibly even give you a cut of the profits).

**The Raffle**

There are certain rules governing the running of raffles of which you ought to be aware. If you are selling tickets at the dance only, drawing the winners and giving the prizes on the same evening, you should be inside the rules as long as you are not giving money prizes – that's illegal. Only the expense of tickets and prizes may be taken out of profit.

If you want more information about running raffles it can be obtained from: The National Council of Social Service, 26 Bedford Square, London, W.C.1.

The prizes may be bought beforehand or donated by interested locals or shopkeepers. If you are buying prizes, you need to keep in mind how many tickets you are likely to sell and then to buy your prizes within the estimated return if you are not to make a loss.

However you obtain your prizes, it is generally better to have a number of prizes rather than just one, or even two. A magnificent display of prizes encourages people to think they have more chance of winning and makes the tickets easier to sell.

Raffle tickets are usually sold in batches, giving people several numbers and more chance of being lucky. It is often simpler to sell the tickets if they are in sheets of five (you can buy books of raffle tickets made up like this) or stapled together in fives. Most stationery shops should sell books of raffle tickets.

It is usual to draw the raffle about half-way through the second half of the evening – perhaps after a vigorous session when everyone needs to sit down for a few minutes to recover! Again, don't forget to ask the band if they would like to join in.

You might like to ask the youngest person present to draw the raffle or, indeed, the oldest, or perhaps you have some important guest in mind for the job. Quite a good way is to have each prize-winner draw a ticket for the next prize.

It never fails to astonish us how often raffle tickets are drawn which no one appears to have bought! The usual procedure when this happens is to call the number three times, and if it is still not claimed, then draw again.

**What Else?**

Perhaps we ought to say a word or two to those who feel that rather than do the actual calling themselves and provide the music off their own bat, they would sooner find a professional caller and band.

We have left this until last for this is really a book for do-it-yourself enthusiasts, but if you *are* going to have help, then it is really one of the first items of preparation to which you will need to give thought.

Unfortunately there is still a real shortage both of professional callers who understand the idiom, and of bands who can play the right sort of music for a barn dance. Those that are available are therefore so much in demand that – for Fridays and Saturdays, anyway – they are likely to be booked up months ahead.

So, if this is the way you are going to do it, you will have to plan well in advance, finding a day when your caller, band and hall are all three available.

Perhaps, at this stage, we ought to say that whatever music you use at a public function, whether it is performed 'live' or on records, it will be under copyright, and before the event you will need to obtain the necessary permission to use it.

In the case of 'live' music, permission may be obtained from

The Performing Right Society, Ltd.,
29 Berners Street,
London, W.1.

In the case of charities the fee may be waived. Your band may be able to advise you about this.

In the case of recorded music, approval should be obtained from

Phonographic Performance, Ltd.,
62 Oxford Street,
London, W.1.

Again, a fee may not be charged in the case of charities if full details are given.

It may seem a little hard to have to pay again for records you have already bought anyway, but do remember you are making use of somebody else's work and they are entitled to some reward for their efforts.

You may not know of a caller or band locally or, indeed, of anyone who can put you in touch with one. If you are looking for a traditional English barn-dance or a barn dance with some traditional square dancing, then The English Folk Song and Dance Society might be able to help you – you will find the addresses of their regional offices later in the book (page 126). If you are looking for a modern American Square Dance, then try the British Association of American Square Dance Clubs, or the Callers Club of Great Britain, whose addresses are also given (page 126).

Callers don't always work with the same band, or bands with the same caller, but they each have their particular favourites and usually, if you approach a caller he will find you a band, or vice versa. If you are able to offer a number of alternative dates, you will probably get fixed up sooner.

The fee which you will have to pay your caller and band will have to be negotiated. It usually depends upon a number of things – the size of the band you require, on which night of the week you want them to play, how long you want them to play for, how far you are asking them to travel, whether you want them to provide amplification, the size of the function, and, of course, the quality of the article.

Generally speaking, you can expect to get what you pay for. If a caller and band are booked months ahead, they have a reputation which is worth paying for and they are likely to charge in relation to this. If you pay only a nominal fee, then it is quite likely you will get a nominal performance.

If you feel unable to afford both caller and band, you might be able to find a caller who works with recorded music, but there are not many of these.

Having engaged your caller, you will turn over the whole evening to him. See that he knows exactly what you have in mind for the evening before he starts; tell him the time of your interval, the time you want to finish your dancing and whether you have any special items (raffle, presentations, talks, etc.) during the evening. He will find the most appropriate moment to include them.

If someone is going to make a short (and it should be *short*) speech of thanks at the end – and this is quite usual – ask the caller for the right time to do it.

If you yourself are making the speech of thanks at the end, and you have had a good time, don't forget to thank the band and caller, even if you are paying them. They'll be much more likely to come again.

**The Big Night**

So it has come. If you have engaged a band and caller, this was probably some time ago, so you should have sent them a card to remind them of the date a couple of weeks beforehand. The tickets have all been sold, the refreshments have all been prepared, your hall has been decorated and the raffle prizes are all on display. The doors have been unlocked thirty minutes beforehand, someone is collecting tickets at the door and there you are awaiting the arrival of the band and caller.

You may already have planned where you want the band to play, but take their advice – the stage might not in fact be the best place as far as the acoustics go, and they will know. Wherever they play, they will almost certainly need a power socket for their amplification, and, if the socket is not near to where the band is to be, a long lead.

Now all you have to do is to give the caller a note of how you want the programme to go (if you are calling yourself, you should have it worked out anyway) and go and join the welcoming committee at the door.

A welcoming committee is a good idea if you have a number of guests, invited or otherwise, who are unfamiliar with the building. It is nice for the guests to feel they are wanted and that someone is there to steer them in the right direction when they arrive.

If you have done your 'P.R.' properly, everybody should now be arriving for, unlike an 'ordinary' dance where usually nothing begins until an hour after the advertised starting time, a barn dance should begin at the announced time with everyone raring to go.

From now on the programme is yours (or the caller's) and what you decide to do and which dances you use, only you will be able to decide in the light of your numbers and their experience. The chapter on the dances will have helped you here.

Towards the end of the evening, you will need to say all your thank-yous – make a list so you don't miss anyone by mistake – but don't leave it right to the end, for you want your dance to finish with a bang, with the dancers roaring for more, and not on a note of polite applause.

If you have engaged a caller you will, at some point, have to pay him. Put the fee in an envelope and hand it over at some quiet moment during the evening – it can be embarrassing for both caller and organizer to be counting over money just as everyone is thanking them for the good time. It is even more embarrassing for the caller to have to ask for his fee before he leaves because nobody has remembered to give it to him!

Chapter 6

# Yourself as caller

Let's say that you have decided to be the caller for the evening.

As we said in Chapter 4, if you are using this book just for your Christmas party with a few friends in the front room, for a laugh, then prop the book up on the piano and enjoy yourselves.

But if you are making your dance a public, or even semi-public, occasion, then you have a very definite responsibility to your customers. They may not be your *paying* customers, they may be just your friends, but you still have a responsibility to them if you want them to remain your friends. Really, you shouldn't attempt a public occasion until you have some experience in the actual dancing.

People will look to you, entirely, for their confidence so you must exude confidence yourself. Not just confidence in your knowledge, but confidence in your appearance, your manner, your voice, the way you handle your dancers, the way you deal with the band or the way you use your record player. This chapter is to help you gain that confidence.

**Dress**

If the 'do' to which you are going is in fancy dress of one sort or another, then try to make the effort to help the evening along by dressing-up yourself. It is not necessary to go to great lengths – unless you want to of course – to obtain the right effect. A coloured shirt with a boy-scout style neckerchief would do for a 'cowboy' dance, a striped blazer for a 'twenties' affair. As long as you can be seen to have made the effort, as they have, the customers will be pleased. Most dances, however, aren't fancy-dress occasions.

If the guests are not dressing-up then neither should you. It is as well to find out what sort of affair it is likely to be before you go, so that you don't turn up in casual clothes and find everyone else in evening dress. Once you know, try to conform and, at the same time, to look as presentable as you can. Even if it says 'casual wear' on the tickets, it won't be appreciated if you turn up wearing the grubby sweater you use for sailing!

**Be Early**

There are a number of reasons why you should be there before everyone else.

Firstly, they will be relying on you for the whole evening's entertainment and will be worried until they see you arrive – full of confidence – to remove the burden from their shoulders.

Then you have a number of points which you will need to see to before the dance begins:

1. Decide where in the hall you will work.
2. Find the power sockets for the amplification – or where the microphone is, if it is a fitted sytem.
3. Set up any apparatus you may be using.
4. Discuss with the band any 'special' music you want them to play.
5. Discuss with the organizers any special points in the evening's programme.
6. Have the music going at the advertised starting time to create an atmosphere, even if there are not enough people to start the dance.

Just how soon you will be able to make a start with the actual dancing depends on just how soon people arrive in any sort of numbers, but however late they may be you should be ready to start at the advertised time. Start just as soon as you have enough for your first dance.

**The P.A. (Public Address System)**

Some callers prefer not to use microphones and do all their calling 'from the floor', perhaps as they themselves are dancing. This is fine, if you are confident that you can do both at once and you are sure your voice can stand the strain. If you are not sure, then you need some form of public address equipment.

There may already be a system fitted in the hall, or you may take along your own. Professional callers often have their own special systems, custom-built to their own requirements, but it is possible to get by with the minimum of equipment.

**Voice Amplification**

Put very simply, amplification of voice needs three items of equipment which might be separate, or partially housed together:

1. A microphone which picks up the noise and turns it into weak electrical currents.

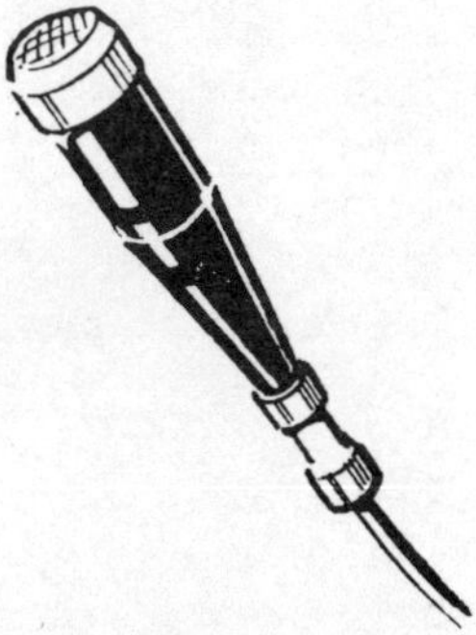

*Hand Microphone*

2. An amplifier which amplifies these weak electrical currents. (This may be a separate purpose-built amplifier or it could be a record player or a tape-recorder – both of which contain amplifiers.)

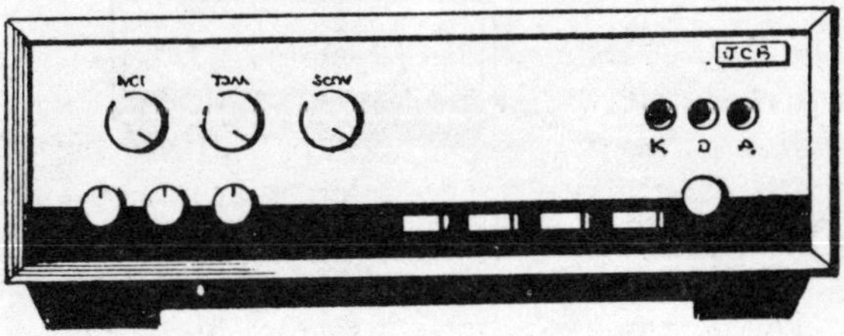

*Separate Amplifier*

3. A loudspeaker(s) which turns the amplified electrical currents back into the original sounds. (The loudspeaker might be built into the record player or tape recorder.)

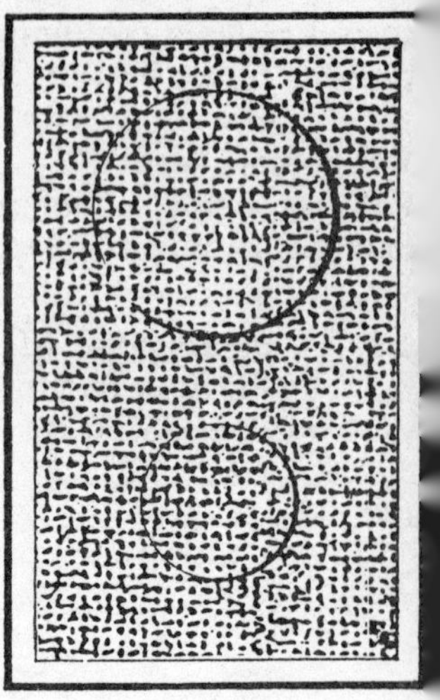

*Loudspeaker*

The three are connected together like this:

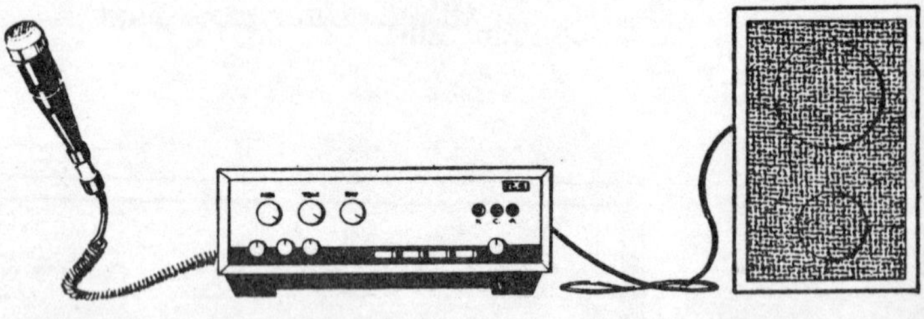

*Microphone* *Amplifier* *Loudspeaker*

If you have, or can obtain, a set-up like this, fine – go ahead and use it. If not, you might be able to make do with a microphone and tape-recorder, like this:

*Tape Recorder* Contains amplifier and loudspeaker.

Most tape-recorders (but not all) can be used in this fashion. Some gramophones – particularly those in use in schools – can also be used in this way.

An even better way of using a tape-recorder as part of a P.A. system is to use it with a large extension speaker which, being larger, is more able to cope with the volume of sound you require.

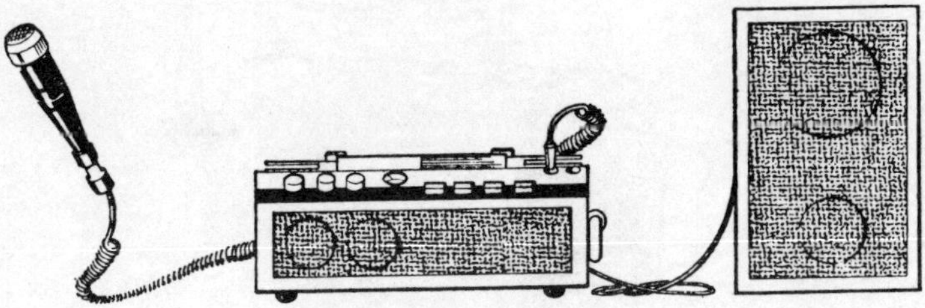

*Tape Recorder* *Loudspeaker*

Most tape recorders, but again not all, have a facility for connecting an extension loudspeaker.

**Using P.A. Equipment**

The P.A. system is your insurance against not being heard easily and clearly by everyone in the hall, but no matter how good your system might be, if you use it incorrectly you may as well not have bothered to pay the premium.

Assuming that your system is in good working order and properly set up, and that you are using it correctly, you will be heard.

**Setting Up**

Loudspeakers must, of course, be set up so that the sound coming from them is directed towards the main body of the hall at about head-height to the dancers. The obvious place, then, would be at the centre-front of the stage, but as the performance of the system can be adversely affected by having the microphone too close to the loudspeaker and you will be using the microphone in the centre of the stage, a better place is at the side of the stage, angled slightly across the hall.

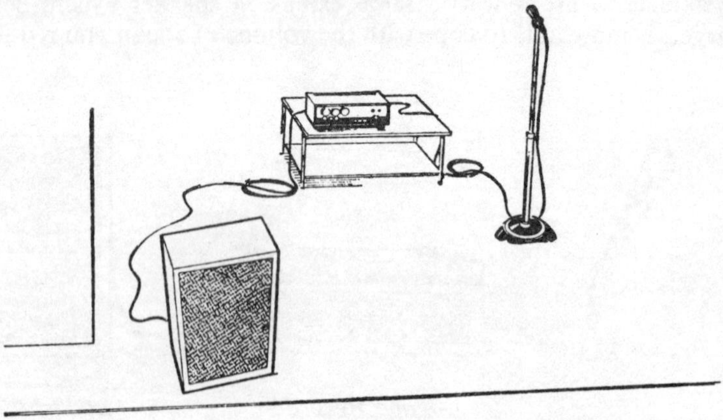

**Microphone Howl (Feed-Back)**

Everybody must be familiar with this noise which, at its best, adds a ringing sound to the amplified voice and at its worst produces a high-pitched howling noise.

It is caused by the amplified sound leaving the loudspeaker, finding its way back into the microphone to be amplified again by the amplifier which sends it out again to come back again, in a vicious circle of sound. It is usually entirely unnecessary and can be avoided if two simple rules are followed:

1. The microphone should not be used in front of, or too near to, the loudspeaker.
2. The volume control on the amplifier should be turned down to a point below that at which the howl sets in.

There are other causes of feed-back – cupping the microphone with the hands, or holding it close to the body. Too much bass or treble on the amplifier control is another cause, but almost always the cause is either or both (1) and (2) above.

It is possible, if necessary, to use the microphone to the side of the actual 'line of fire' of the loudspeaker, but this is better not done unless you know that this will not cause your system to misbehave.

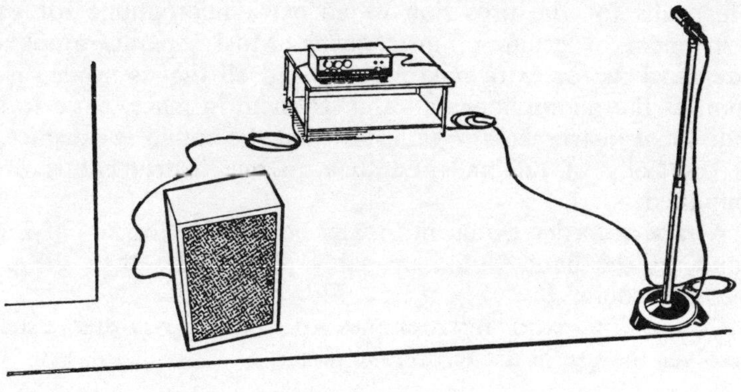

## Using the Microphone

A microphone is a delicate instrument and doesn't take kindly to mishandling – and with some microphones this includes 'blowing' on them. If possible, always have a stand on which to rest it, even if you hold it in your hand while you are using it.

If your system is working correctly, your voice will be picked up and amplified quite adequately without the need for you to talk in anything other than your usual voice. Many people make the mistake of thinking that they have to shout into a microphone to be heard. Don't try to do the amplifier's job – all you will succeed in doing is distorting your voice so that no one will be able to distinguish what you are saying.

The microphone should be approximately twelve inches away from the mouth and your normal speaking voice is the one to use. The volume setting on the amplifier can be determined when you set everything up before anyone arrives, although you may need to increase this just a *little* when eveyone is in and the dance is going strong.

At the same time as you are setting your volume level, test the speaker situations to make sure you can be heard equally well all over the hall.

## Amplification of Music

### *With a Band*

This calls for the provision of an extra microphone for each instrument or group of instruments. Most separate amplifiers have sockets for extra microphones and all that is needed is to connect the microphones up and set them in place, close to the individual instruments. Again, test that the sound is satisfactory in the body of the hall and that no one instrument is over-amplified.

A tape recorder would not really be suitable for amplifying a band, as the band would probably play louder than the tape recorder could.

Connecting extra microphones to a tape recorder usually involves the use of a microphone mixer.

*Recorded Music*

A record player is basically the same as the amplification set-up outlined above. It has two of the parts – amplifier and loudspeaker – already mentioned. There is a difference in that the original weak electrical currents, instead of being supplied by a microphone, come from the stylus on the playing arm.

Most record-players are made for use in an average-size room in which excessive volume would be unacceptable. The player that sounds very loud in your sitting room becomes remarkably docile in a large hall. If your hall is not too big and your crowd not too large, your player might cope. If you are planning a big event, then it might be as well to have your record player connected to the amplifier so that it, too, can be made louder. Some record players have the necessary output socket for connecting to a separate amplifier; those that don't can easily be adapted by any competent radio dealer.

Your set-up would then be:

It would be pointless to connect your record player in this way to a tape-recorder, since the tape-recorder can give you no more volume than the record player.

**Using a Record Player**

If possible have a thoroughly competent assistant to look after your records and to play them as you require – you don't want too much to think about.

The way your apparatus is handled will reflect upon your dance. Here are some tips to help you:

The records are easier to handle if you have a record-player which has its turntable and playing arm above the cabinet case:

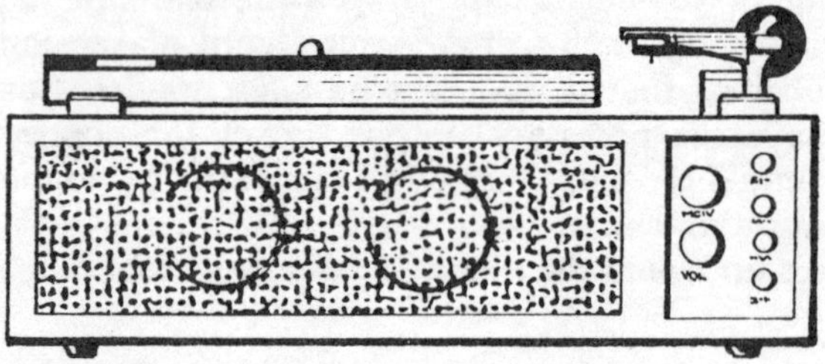

This will not only enable you to see exactly where each track begins and ends but will also make it easier to set down the stylus in the 'space' between the tracks.

No matter how expert you may become at finding the 'space', it is impossible to become 100 per cent accurate so, to avoid broadcasting your false starts to your people, turn down the volume until you find the space between the tracks. Then turn it up again quickly so that everyone hears the beginning of the tune. Use this method whenever you set down the arm. Reverse the procedure when you take it off.

An automatic player should be avoided if possible. Not only do these have a long spindle and the associated record-holding gear above the turntable – all calculated to get in the way when you are in a hurry – but they also have an annoying habit of tripping the arm and switching off just as you are trying to lower the arm on to an inside track.

It goes without saying, of course, that you must be completely familiar with the discs you are using – you must know which records are suitable for which dances, which tracks are on which discs, how many times a particular tune is played through (write it on the sleeve, if you can't remember). You should also know just when the tune is being played through for the last time on a track.

It is very difficult to count the tunes through while a dance is under way. It is also unnecessary, for usually there is some way of telling which is the last time through. Maybe the band returns to the original tune, or it may be that you can recognize the end by the way in which the music is played the last time through. Play your records over and over again until you are able to say exactly when they are ending.

**The Public Use of Records**

You will not have forgotten, as mentioned earlier, that if you are using gramophone records at a public occasion you should have first obtained the permission of Phonographic Performance, Ltd. (See page 107.)

**At the Dance**

The overall form of the evening is in the hands of the organizers, of course – unless they have entirely turned it over to you as caller. But the dance part is yours – that's why you were invited – and you ought to be quite clear in your mind just how you are going to make the evening go.

Earlier in this book we mentioned that a caller was a teacher in disguise and that a good teacher always sounded like a friend.

Of course you are going to teach, but the moment you let it appear that you are teaching you will kill completely any atmosphere you have built up. Remember, above all, that your customers are there to have a good time and that everything else comes second. There are a number of ways in which a caller can kill off the atmosphere.

1. Assuming that people have come to be lectured.
2. Assuming that people know more than they do.

3. Trying to get people to 'run' before they can 'walk'.
4. Presenting material poorly.
5. Being impatient.

**1. The Lecture**

People have come to dance and to have a good time while they are doing so. You may think it interesting to know where the word 'allemande' has its derivation or the origin of a particular dance. They won't care a bit. Save your fund of knowledge for when you are asked to deliver a lecture. Get on with the action!

**2. How Much Do They Know?**

Nothing. Not even their right hands from their left – and even if you succeed in teaching everybody *that* during the evening, you've done something. And don't assume that just because you have been to them before, they will remember a word of what you did on the last occasion! (But don't let them feel that you're more clever than they are.)

**3. Go Slowly**

To people who have no knowledge at all – not even of where they should stand when making up a set – a dance such as 'Waves of Tory' is a long, complicated and difficult series of things to do. You may find it exciting to dance – they may find it terrifying.

If you plan your programme so that each succeeding dance introduces only a minimum of new material, people will take this in their stride without actually realizing they *are* learning all the time.

**4. Poor Presentation**

Think about the difficulties of each figure (as we have outlined them) and try to show your dances so that it is quite clear what you are asking people to do.

**5. Be Patient**

Impatience is the cardinal sin. They may be making a noise, they may seem incredibly stupid, but whatever you may think, don't let it show in your voice or on your face. The customer is always right (and never stupid).

**Planning a Programme**

We have put the dances in Chapter 4 roughly in order of difficulty, but only you can be the judge of how things are going and when you want a good romp and when you want to ease off the pace. Only you can be the judge of what is the learning pace of your people and if you are stimulating their imagination or if you are insulting their intelligence.

However, to help you, and to illustrate what we have said about introducing the minimum amount of new material with each succeeding dance, let us give you the sort of lines on which we would work.

Bear in mind that this is a suggested method, not a hard and fast plan of action and, although it refers only to the dances in this book, your programme could well include any of the dozens of dances contained in other folk publications. (See p. 127.)

**The First Dance of the Evening**

If everyone arrived at the same time, you could begin with the whole crowd and work along from there, but this seldom happens and whatever you begin with will be missed by the large majority. People will be arriving all the time and it is a good idea to begin with a dance which is not dependent upon a fixed number of couples and which people can join at any stage, as they come in.

**The Big Set**

This is an ideal dance to begin with. It has no set pattern and you can vary it to suit the learning pace of your crowd, repeating any figures which they find difficult to pick up, and moving on to others when everyone has got the 'hang' of it.

Try to encourage new arrivals as they come in and don't hesitate to stop once or twice to give them an opportunity if they seem loath to join in.

The *Big Set* will also show you just how quickly or slowly you will be able to go through the rest of the evening. If they are able to pick up your calls and interpret them into action quickly, you'll be able to progress fairly quickly. If not, then you must adjust your pace accordingly.

Don't be afraid of repetition. It may be boring to you but to them it is an adventure into the unknown and an exciting one at that. Let them see that you find it so, too.

By the time the *Big Set* comes to an end, you should have managed to show them a number of the basic figures which you will be using throughout the evening. These could include the right and left hand turns, do-si-do, swing, promenade, circle left and right, in and out.

**The Virginia Reel**

If, in your *Big Set*, you have introduced all the usual figures – as set out above and in the dance on page 41, your second dance could well be the *Virginia Reel*. This has nothing in it which you have not already shown everyone, except the down and back figure.

More people will probably have arrived in between the dances and it will not be safe to assume that everyone who comes into the sets for this dance will have already danced your *Big Set*, so walk it through, as we have suggested. You will now have a core of 'experienced' dancers who will know what a right hand turn and a left hand turn are and your new arrivals will pick up the figures from them.

**Lucky Seven**

Again this contains only one figure which your dancers will not already have done – the chain. But, again, don't assume that all of your dancers will necessarily have danced the *Big Set* and the *Virginia Reel*. Some, more timid than the rest, will sit and watch for a while. They may have watched what everyone else has been doing but this doesn't mean that they will be up with the others who have actually been dancing. Walk it all for them.

**A Sicilian Circle**

This dance takes another small step forward, with its right and left hand star. A star is two separate hand-turns, one above the other, so this is only a small step. The progression to the next couple is really a promenade.

By now your dance will be well under way. You have danced in a circle formation, in a Sicilian circle formation and in sets. You might like to continue this variety of pattern by changing to a square formation.

**Coming Round the Mountain**

All the figures in this dance have already been danced earlier in the evening. The new formation is enough for your folk to contend with and because you are not asking too much of them at once, they will be able to follow the dance and will quickly gain confidence.

**And So On**

Remember this is not a set pattern – you can follow the same principles, using any number of different dances. And you can always add in a few Old Time couple dances, such as the Veleta, St Bernard's Waltz, Gay Gordons, etc.

Remember, they will be relying entirely on you and looking to you to hold their hands, as it were. Don't make each dance an assault course of new formations, new figures, and new rhythms which will confuse and discourage your dancers.

Look for 'platforms of learning' and when you have moved everyone up a step, don't hesitate to repeat and consolidate your platform before you move to the next one, if necessary. Never ask too much of your dancers in any one bite.

You'll soon find out whether you have asked too much of your dancers – everyone, even the most experienced caller, does from time to time. But what is important is that you sit down after the evening is over and you have recovered your breath and try to think how the next time will be better.

And there will certainly be a next time if you have played your part well.

So, there it is! Good luck with your first dance.

And the next.

And the next!

# Appendix

**For Further Advice**
In this book we have used only figures and dances which the layman with no experience can easily understand and assimilate. There are, as we have said, many, many dances, both English and American, which we have not mentioned. There are also many, many figures which we have not mentioned.

We hope that we will have given you some taste for our traditional style dancing and that you might now like to learn more about some of them. Fortunately, wherever you live in Britain, there is someone not too far away who can help you find out how you might take it further.

All of these societies will be pleased to help you in any way – in finding a band or caller, in running an evening or maybe in taking it even further. If you want advice, they'll be pleased to help you. Here are some addresses:

**Useful Addresses**
(1) English Folk Dance and Song Society, Cecil Sharp House, 2 Regent's Park Road, London, NW1 7AY.

with Regional Offices at
- (*a*) Eastern Region Office: High View, Ashfield Green, Wickhambrook, Newmarket, Suffolk.
- (*b*) Midland Region Office: 75, Green Lane, Kettering, Northants NN15 0DA
- (*c*) Northern Region Office: 5, Norfolk Mount, Chapel Allerton, Leeds L57 PU.
- (*d*) Western Region Office: The Folk House, 10, Richmond Road, Exeter EX4 4JA.

(2) The British Association of American Square Dance Clubs, Hon. Sec. Miss Pat Robinson, 34 Chaucer House, Churchill Gardens, Pimlico, London, S.W.1.

(3) The Callers Club of Great Britain, Hon. Sec. D. Taylor, 5 Quinton Close, Churchdown, Glos.

(4) The Royal Scottish Country Dance Society, Hon. Sec. Miss M. Gibson, 12 Coates Crescent, Edinburgh, EH3 7AF. London Sec. Mr. H. G. Draper, 43, Rochester Road, Northwood Hills, Middlesex.

(5) The Society for International Folk Dancing, Hon. Sec. Miss E. Foster, 33, Orchard Avenue, Southgate, London, N.14 4NB.

(6) The Welsh Folk Dance Society, Hon. Sec. Mrs. J. Huw Jones, Dolawenydd, Betws, Ammanford, Dyfed SA18 2HE.

The EFDSS publishes an annual Folk Directory which gives hundreds of useful addresses.

**Music**
*Books of Tunes*
*English*
The Charlton Memorial Tune Book of Northumbrian Tunes (The Northumbrian Pipers Society, 135 Sydney Grove, Newcastle-upon-Tyne, 4)

The Fiddlers Tune Book, 1 (EFDSS)
Popular Selections of Dance Airs, Books 1, 2, 3 and 4 (EFDSS)

*American*

American Tunes for Squares and Contras, Books 1 and 2 (EFDSS)
American Square Dance Tunes (EFDSS)

*Scottish*

Kerr's Collections (James Kerr, 79 Berkeley Street, Glasgow, C2)
The Scottish Violinist (Bayley and Ferguson, 79 Berkeley Street, Glasgow, C2)

*Irish*

The Irish Fiddler (Mozart Allen, 84 Carlton Place, Glasgow, C5)
O'Neill's Collection (Waltons Music Ltd, 15 New Bond Street, London, W1)

**Other Books of Folk Dance Instructions and Tunes**

*English*

Community Dances Manuals 1 to 7 (EFDSS)*
Everyday Dances (EFDSS)
English Folk Dancing for Schools and Junior Youth Clubs (EFDSS)
English Folk Dancing in the Primary School (EFDSS)*
Swing Partners (Novello & Co. Ltd, 3 Upper James Street, London W1)
Dancing for Fun (Talking Books, see record list)
Know the Game – English Folk Dancing (EP Publishing)*
Maypole Dances (Curwen Press)

*Playford Type*

The Country Dance Book – New Series (EFDSS)
Set and Honour (Novello & Co. Ltd, 3 Upper James Street, London W1)

*American*

The Ralph Page Book of Contras (EFDSS)

*Irish*

The Irish Folk Dance Books (Paterson's Publications Ltd, 36 Wigmore Street, London W1)

*Scottish*

The Scottish Country Dance Books (Paterson's Publications Ltd, 36 Wigmore Street, London, W1)

*Welsh*

Come and Dance (University of Wales Press)

*Companion records (see page 128)

**Useful Records**

Quite honestly, any record of suitable length and rhythm may be used for your dancing. Many of the English dances can be danced just as well to Scottish records and so on. Whatever you use, make sure it has a good lively rhythm and is tuneful.

Beware of buying records without hearing them right through first. Records which contain a dozen tracks may have only one track suitable for your purpose.

Records are withdrawn from the list when they cease to sell. Here are some records currently (1980) in the lists which you might find suitable.

**Folk Dance Records**

*English*

Let's Dance Country-Style (The Southerners) LDS12* (see below)
Dancing for Fun Series 1 to 5 (EFDSS) DFF1–5 (Instruction book with record, caller on the record.)
Barn Dance One (EFDSS) BR1 }
Barn Dance Two (EFDSS) BR2 } instructions on the sleeve.
English Folk Dancing (The Southerners) KTG12*
English Folk Dancing in the Primary School (EFDSS) BR3*
English Folk Dancing for Young Folk (EFDSS) BR5
Community Dance Records 1,2,5,6 (EFDSS) CDM1 CDM2 CDM5 CDM6*
English Folk Dancing, J. Shand (EMI One Up) OU2015

*Companion Book – see book-list.

*American*

| | | |
|---|---|---|
| Enjoy Yourself, Friendly Style | (GUS Records) JDC0079 | All with caller on the record and instructions on the sleeve. |
| Two Change-partner Square Dances | (GUS Records) JDC0080 | |
| Colour it, Friendly-style | (GUS Records) JDC0081 | |
| Himazas and others | (GUS Records) JDC0082 | |

The Southerners play Ralph Page (EFDSS) RP500

*Playford Dances*

The English Dancing Master 1,2,3 (EFDSS) PLA 1,2,3

All music, records and books mentioned above are obtainable from the English Folk Dance and Song Society (address above). Catalogues with additional material are available free on application.

*Let's Dance Country Style with the Southerners*

SOUTHERNERS LDS 12 (disc) Southerners LDS 12T (tape cassette)

This record matches the Book exactly for dances 6 to 17; with 12 tracks recorded specifically to complement the book. The first five dances have music available on records DFF1 & DFF2, also recorded by Southerners on EFDSS label.

Obtainable from The Folk Shop, 2 Regents Park Road, London, NW1 7AY.